Tales from
MISERY RIDGE

One man's adventures
in the great outdoors

by Paul J. Fournier

Also from Islandport Press

Where Cool Waters Flow by Randy Spencer

My Life in the Maine Woods by Annette Jackson

Nine Mile Bridge by Helen Hamlin

Old Maine Woman by Glenna Johnson Smith

Abbott's Reach by Ardeana Hamlin

Shoutin' into the Fog by Thomas Hanna

Contentment Cove and *Young* by Miriam Colwell

Stealing History and *Breaking Ground* by William D. Andrews

Windswept, Mary Peters, and *Silas Crockett* by Mary Ellen Chase

In Maine by John N. Cole

The Cows Are Out! by Trudy Chambers Price

Hauling by Hand by Dean Lawrence Lunt

A Moose and a Lobster Walk into a Bar by John McDonald

At One: In a Place Called Maine by Lynn Plourde
and Leslie Mansmann

The Cat at Night by Dahlov Ipcar

My Wonderful Christmas Tree by Dahlov Ipcar

Farmyard Alphabet by Dahlov Ipcar

These and other Maine books are available at:
www.islandportpress.com

Tales from
MISERY RIDGE

One man's adventures
in the great outdoors

by Paul J. Fournier

ISLANDPORT PRESS

Islandport Press
P.O. Box 10
Yarmouth, Maine 04096
www.islandportpress.com
books@islandportpress.com

ISBN: 978-1-934031-60-5
Library of Congress Card Number: 2011935471

Book jacket design by Karen F. Hoots / Hoots Design
Book designed by Michelle A. Lunt / Islandport Press
Publisher Dean L. Lunt
Cover image by Paul J. Fournier courtesy of
   Maine State Museum

To my dear wife Lorraine, who daily supports me and tolerates my grumpy-old-man phase;

And to my dearly departed wife Anita, who shared years of adventures.

I am twice blessed.

Table of Contents

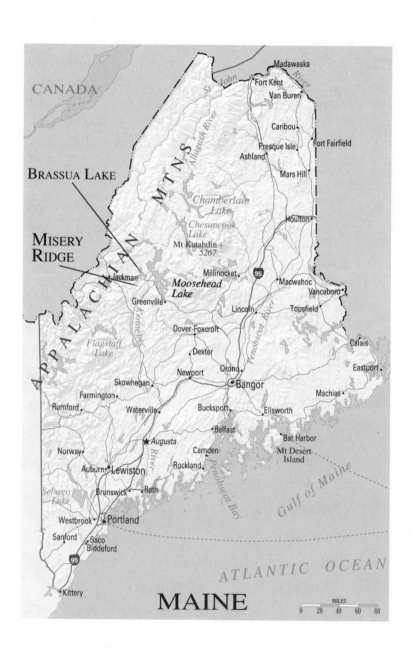

CANADA

Madawaska
Fort Kent
Van Buren

Caribou
Presque Isle — Fort Fairfield
Ashland
Mars Hill

BRASSUA LAKE

Chamberlain Lake
Chesuncook Lake
Mt Katahdin + 5267

Houlton

MISERY RIDGE

Jackman
Millinocket
95
Macwahoc
Vanceboro

Moosehead Lake

Greenville
Lincoln
Topsfield

Dover-Foxcroft

Calais

Flagstaff Lake
Dexter

Eastport

Newport
Orono
Bangor

Skowhegan

Farmington
Machias

Rumford
Waterville
Bucksport
Ellsworth

Belfast

Norway
Augusta
Camden
Bar Harbor
Mt Desert Island

Auburn Lewiston
Rockland

Sebago Lake
Brunswick
Bath

Penobscot Bay

Gulf of Maine

Westbrook
Portland

Sanford
Saco
Biddeford

95

ATLANTIC OCEAN

Kittery

MAINE

MILES
0   20   40   60   80

Introduction

Misery Ridge, despite its sinister name, is a hand-some, if modest, natural feature. Its highest point, Misery Knob, is but 2,128 feet above sea level. It is located in Misery Township, an unincorporated town located west of Moosehead Lake in Somerset County, Maine. It comprises 21,963 acres (some thirty-five square miles), primarily woodlands, with a number of ponds, streams, and bogs. It is home to from seventy to one hundred moose (two to three per square mile, biologists estimate), an unknown number of deer and bears, and zero humans.

The name, Misery, is actually a modern-day corruption of a Native American name for the region. Father Sebastian Rale, a Jesuit missionary who lived with the Abenaki Indians for more than thirty years (and was killed in a massacre of an Indian village at Norridgewock in 1724), traveled with them throughout the region. He was famous for having written a dictionary of the Abenaki language. He wrote that to the Abenakis, Misery (earlier, Miseree) meant something like "many things," and he thought it referred to the numerous small ponds—including the Misery Ponds at the source of Misery Stream—that are found there. He also noted that the mouth of Misery Stream, where it empties into Brassua Lake, was well known to the Indians as a good place to camp and catch fish.

Misery Ridge, if you include Blue Ridge, runs in a relatively straight line some fifteen miles southwesterly from the shore of Moosehead Lake at Rockwood. It is, in fact, a continuation (broken by a mile-wide stretch of Moosehead Lake) of the same rocky outcropping of which Mount Kineo is the most famous and spectacular feature. All were shaped and weathered and sculptured by the two-mile-thick mantle of ice that covered them during the Ice Age.

For nearly a decade—from the mid-1950s to the mid-1960s—I lived within sight of Misery Ridge, virtually in its shadow. My memories of that period, far from being miserable, are in fact, for the most part, pleasurable and sweetly nostalgic.

In early 1955, after my discharge from the U.S. Air Force following the Korean Conflict, my late wife, Anita, and I purchased a modest set of "sporting camps" (catering to fishermen, campers, and hunters) on the shore of Brassua Lake. Our view from the front porch of our cabin looked across the lake southwest to Misery Cove, Misery Stream, and, overlooking all, Misery Ridge. It was Misery Ridge I looked up to see in the morning as I began each day, and Misery Ridge that showed me the last rays of the setting sun. I saw and came to deeply appreciate its humble but steadfast beauty in all the seasons: in the soft haze of midsummer; the sharp, crisp days of autumn when it glowed golden and crimson under bright cobalt skies; the steely gray of bare branches and snow-covered evergreens on snowy winter days; and the promising blush of green tide moving up its flanks in the spring. The scene remains deeply etched in my mind. The memory of Misery Ridge's serenity and steadfastness has helped guide me along life's path.

Some of the following stories sprang from the shadows of Misery Ridge; some did not. Those that took place elsewhere in the state represent their own Misery Ridges, if you will, calling to mind an appreciation for Maine's enduring natural wonders and times gone by.

Paul J. Fournier
August 2011

The Seductive Canoe

I was fifteen that summer when first love struck. She was seventeen—seventeen feet long, that is, a gorgeous Old Town canoe, slender, graceful, and sleek. Her green skin shone. Her beautifully curved cedar ribs and planking and white ash gunwales glistened with spar varnish like gold in the sunlight. My heart fluttered whenever my gaze fell upon her.

I was lucky enough, the fifteenth year of my life, to get a job at Camp Winnebago, a summer camp for boys in Fayette, Maine, east of my hometown of Chisholm. One of the privileges I enjoyed that summer was being allowed in the evenings to take the oldest canoe in the camp's fleet out on the lake. I spent many happy hours alone, learning to make the canoe respond to the paddle, and it was this old canoe that I fell in love with.

It was the custom for the camp to retire and sell one or two of the older canoes at the end of the season and replace them. I couldn't stand to part with my paramour. I spent $25—a fair chunk of my earnings—to purchase that beat-up canoe. It became my most prized possession in the world and my best friend. Since I had no wheels of my own, I had my dad drive it to a secluded pond a few miles from home, where I hid it in the woods. Whenever I had some time to spare, I'd hike to the pond.

The canoe became my entry into a new world of discovery. The pond was connected to a miles-long boggy stream that was seldom visited by humans and was home to a variety of wildlife. I spent many long days in that swampy realm and began a lifelong fascination with the wild creatures living in it. I saw my first moose there. I slipped my canoe along silently, as only a canoe can, to watch beavers building their lodges, and mink, muskrat, and otter going about their lives. I observed great blue herons and bitterns, and ospreys catching fish. Some of my acquaintances were afraid of swamps and told me I was foolish to spend time alone in such a "dangerous" place "full of quicksand and snakes!" I never encountered quicksand, though I had to be wary of mucky sinkholes while wading around the bog. There are no poisonous snakes to be concerned about in Maine, but I did occasionally see large, harmless water snakes swimming along.

When autumn arrived, I found the canoe ideal for sneaking up on waterfowl. And, it was excellent for hunting deer. Hunters roaming the surrounding ridges would drive the deer into the swamp, where they'd bed down for the day. The wary deer, accustomed to being watchful for hunters walking in the woods, were apt to be more complacent about being approached from the water.

The Prince

When I was seventeen, I felt the need for a second canoe, a shorter, lighter, more portable craft than my big Old Town, which had accumulated considerable middle-aged weight through moisture and years of paint layers. I greatly admired a canoe that Leon Prince had built for a trapper I met one fall day in my favorite swamp, so I paid the elderly canoe builder a visit in North Monmouth.

Mr. Prince turned out to be a small, genial, lonesome gentleman in oversize overalls. Contrary to the stereotype of taciturn rural Maine folk, he was downright garrulous. He took apparent pleasure in showing me around his cluttered shop in an old barn. He was particularly proud of his large collection of old wood planes, which he still used in his work every day. I'd never before seen a canoe mold, the shaped wooden form on which a wood canoe is assembled. Its ribs were made of iron. After showing me the steam box, Prince explained that the shaped cedar ribs, after being steam-heated in the box, were bent over each of the iron ribs and clamped to the canoe's inner gunwales. Steam-heating the ribs made them easy to bend without breaking and ensured they would hold their shape. "When you fit the plankin' on, and drive the tacks into the ribs, the points strike those iron rib bands and it clinches 'em ovah," he said.

Equally fascinating to me was Mr. Prince's set-up for stretching the canvas over the finished hull. A canvas sling was suspended from the barn rafters. The hull was set into it and pressed down from above by a large jack. When stretched to the proper tautness, the canvas conformed itself smoothly to the canoe hull and was tacked into place along the gunwales and stems. After a trimming, the hull was removed from the jig, and the outer gunwales and other final trim pieces such as thwarts and seats were installed. Finally, a special filling compound was applied to the entire canvas. The compound cured into a hard finish, which was sanded smooth and then painted.

After an enjoyable and informative couple of hours in his shop, I left with Mr. Prince's promise that he'd build a canoe for me. He didn't even ask me, a teenager, for an advance deposit. A month later I returned to North Monmouth and he proudly showed me his latest creation. The price: one hundred dollars. I'd been saving for months. For the first time, I had my very own, brand-new, shiny green canoe.

When I turned eighteen I became a Registered Maine Guide. (Unlike today, when guide applicants must pass rigid tests, all that was required was the signature of the local game warden; since he was familiar with my experience in the outdoors, he evidently felt I was competent.) My first several years of guiding were at Lakewood Camps at Middle Dam on Lower Richardson Lake, one of the Rangeley chain lakes in Western Maine.

Here was a unique little sportsman's paradise, tucked away in a remote corner of the state close by the New Hampshire and Quebec borders. The Richardson Lakes are the lowest, wildest, and least known of the Rangeley chain of lakes. Most of the land around the lakes was then owned by the Brown Paper Company, which operated a mill in Berlin, New Hampshire. The company cut wood in the forests and drove it to the mill on the lakes and the connecting rivers. There was only one gravel road to the extreme southern shore of Lower Richardson Lake, from South Arm. Most of the lake's shoreline was wild and untouched, with only an occasional primitive fishing cottage sprinkled here and there. Fortunately for this neophyte guide, the waters held sizable populations of trout and landlocked salmon.

The Rangeleys at the time, though, were not canoe country. Most fishing was done from the locally evolved "Rangeley boat." The original Rangeley was in fact an adaptation of the canoe, being double-ended and built with narrow ribs and lap-strake planking. It was deeper and wider than a canoe and fitted for rowing rather than paddling. It was too heavy to routinely carry or "portage" on one's shoulders, especially after it had acquired several years of moisture and coats of paint. In time the Rangeley boat was built with a squared stern to accommodate outboard motors. My first year of guiding I owned no outboard, so I did a lot of rowing for my clients. Some traditionalists, in fact, preferred it. I believe we hooked more fish when I rowed than when we used the outboard.

Still, my lightweight Prince canoe served me well at the Lakewood Camps. It could be portaged relatively easily to small ponds for fishing, so it received a bit of "professional" use. Mostly, though, I used it for my own personal pleasure, paddling along the shore on quiet evenings with the woman I would eventually marry.

The White

I was in real canoe country when I moved to Brassua Lake in the Moosehead Lake Region. Canoes have been a vital part of the Moosehead scene for thousands of years. Henry David Thoreau, who made three trips to the Maine woods in the 1840s and '50s, witnessed on two occasions Indians building birch canoes, and he described the process in considerable detail in his journals. Although white men have never been able to improve upon the Indians' basic design of the long, slender, light canoe, in time they developed improvements in materials used to make the canoe more durable and watertight. The first notable change was substituting canvas for birch bark, whose seams required frequent pitching. Wood and canvas were used to build canoes from the late nineteenth century to the later half of the twentieth century This basic wood/canvas canoe dominated canoe building from the late nineteenth century to the latter half of the twentieth century, when the advent of aluminum and, later, Fiberglas, Kevlar, and other petrochemically derived materials again revolutionized the canoe.

But the wood/canvas canoe was the one I grew up with and fell for like a ton of bricks. And it was what the guides around Moosehead Lake and the Moose River were using when I moved there in the mid-fifties. The favored guide canoe was the twenty-foot White, built by the E. M. White Company of Old Town (located, in fact, just down the street from its giant rival, Old Town Canoe Company, and since assimilated by Old Town, which still builds a brand of White canoe). The White was a sturdy, honest craft that handled the rolling waves of huge Moosehead as well as the rapids on the Moose and other nearby rivers with equal authority. It had a relatively flat bottom but no keel, which left it susceptible to sideslipping in a crosswind on the lake. That, however, worked in its favor when running rapids, when it is sometimes necessary to "ferry" or slide the canoe sideways to avoid rocks. The White canoe was built very much along the lines of the Indians' classic birch, with low bow and stern. This was a distinct advantage over higher-prowed canoes in the wind.

When I began working with the Moosehead guides I soon acquired a White. Though I'd been handling canoes for a decade, I found I had much to learn. The guides, most considerably older than I, had quite a few canoeing tricks of which I'd not been aware, and they weren't necessarily anxious to share them with a novice from "down south" (even if only south of

Moosehead). I had to learn mostly by observing and listening to their casual conversations.

As with many other aspiring canoeists, I had learned the basic sternman's paddling motion, the "J" stroke. This maneuver has been taught at canoeing schools and summer camps for decades. Thousands of canoeists use it. Other strokes also are taught, including the draw, pry, and sweep, and all are useful at certain times, but the "J" is fundamental, and I was rather proud of my mastery of it. But somehow I was finding it difficult to keep up with the grizzled guides in their forties, fifties, and even sixties, especially so on windy days on the lake. I was then in my mid-twenties, lean and hard and, I thought, in good physical condition, but these geezers were embarrassing me. It was downright humbling.

After I had guided for several months, a couple of the older guides thawed a bit and seemed to be tolerating me. I became the butt of some good-natured ribbing. One noon as I arrived at the lunch ground—perhaps showing off a bit my flair for paddling—one of my new pals, Ed King (he became one of my best friends among the guides), poked Bud Pelkey in the ribs and shouted at me: "That's a nice Charles River stroke you've got there, Paul!" Several other guides nearby broke out in big grins; they were too polite to laugh outright. Then and there I vowed to find out what their paddling secret was. I became a keen observer; as surreptitiously as possible, I followed the other guides and watched from afar.

The J-stroke paddler extends both arms forward to "grab" a paddleful of water and pull it back toward the stern. This tends to shove the bow to the opposite side. As the stroke nears its rearward limit, the paddle handle is twisted so that the blade is parallel to the canoe, and the blade pushed out to the side and used as a rudder to steer the canoe back into line. This means the canoe is constantly wobbling, if ever so imperceptibly. It requires a lot of energy—much of it expended wastefully to steer the canoe back into line with each stroke. And it puts considerable strain on arm, shoulder, and chest muscles.

It gradually began to dawn upon me that the guides were using the paddle in a different, and evidently more efficient, manner. Instead of reaching out with both arms, they kept the lower hand low down on the shaft, outside the canoe, close to the blade and relatively still, using it more as a fulcrum or pivot point. Oftentimes they slid the paddle along the gunwale. The upper hand was often held flat against the wide part of the handle rather than curled over the top, and provided most of the power. In fact, the paddler's back was put into use to push the top of the handle, rather than pulling with the arms. The stroke was normally fairly short. And as the paddle blade came rearward, a slight twist was imparted, which kept the bow from veering and negated the need for the exaggerated "J" or hook at the end of the stroke. The blade barely cleared the water as it was brought forward. Result: a shorter, more-efficient pad-dling stroke, less wasteful of energy and ideally suited to a lone stern paddler. In their idle conversations, I noted that these guides seldom spoke of paddling, but of "pushing" a canoe.

Gradually, I began practicing what I observed. I never attained the natural proficiency of those who had grown up using this technique, but I found that by using my back to push the paddle, rather than pulling, and not needing to lift the pad-dle high, I had less pain and fatigue in my arms and shoulders after a long day in the canoe. And less difficulty and embar-rassment in keeping up with the oldsters.

Paul Fournier poles his canoe up Allagash Stream.

But, I soon found out, paddling was only half the job of propelling a canoe. Poling was the other. Poling upstream is usually resorted to when the current is swift, and the water is from one foot to, say, three or four feet deep. Indians poled their canoes upstream since time immemorial, and before the advent of the outboard motor, white men capitalized upon the method with only minor innovations. Chiefly, they put an iron shoe on the end of the pole to prolong its life.

Again, poling is a skill acquired only after considerable practice. And, it's dangerous. Poling is done while standing and poles can slip on smooth rock or ledge, causing the poler to suddenly lurch to one side, the canoe to the other. Poles also can get stuck between rocks and, if the poler isn't alert, agile, and swift, can pitchpole him head over heels. Poles can also break, in which case the canoe can instantly be swept sideways in the current and dumped. (Please, don't ask how I know all

13

this.) In all cases, the canoeist at the very least gets wet; in some cases, drowned.

The canoe pole, at least in Maine, is called a setting pole, perhaps because it is "set" against the bottom of the river. (There's a yarn about the fellow who applied for a job as game warden with the Maine Department of Inland Fisheries and Wildlife. One of the questions on the test was: What is a setting pole? His reply: "It's the pole a warden climbs and sets on to watch for poachers.") When the river became too deep, or the rapids too swift and turbulent for poling, the guides could choose to either "track" (upstream) or "line" (downstream) the lightened canoe from shore using long ropes attached yoke-fashion to control the canoe. Or, they might opt for the final resort, to physically carry or "portage" the canoe and camp duffel around the rapids.

Once again, I had to learn poling through observing, mimicking, and practicing. Through trial and (lots of) error (let's not get too specific!), I began to acquire certain knowledge and skills: The canoe should always be kept slightly higher at the upstream end, whether the bow, going up, or stern going down; keeping the bow a few degrees off-center of the current flow makes it possible to use the pole against its force to help keep the canoe headed straight; keep the pole close to the side of the canoe; once the pole is set, "climb" it hand over hand; keep the knees bent and body slightly bowed to absorb shocks; allow the canoe to weathercock into the current to realign itself. Above all, don't get caught crossways in the current—it can dump you or wrap your canoe around a rock. All of this needs to be kept in mind under conditions that can vary daily or even hourly: high or low water; tricky, gusty winds; light or heavy loads.

A lightly loaded canoe, of course, is easiest to pole; it slides over the surface. You can shift the trim by simply stepping forward or back in the big canoe. (By the way, poling is best done in longer canoes, from seventeen to twenty feet; normal pole length is eleven to twelve feet.) Poling becomes more difficult when you take on passengers. One person sitting in the bow is fairly reasonable. Two riders make it exponentially more difficult. The canoe, instead of riding and slipping over the water, now digs into it, and it is more difficult to trim the canoe, especially going upstream. But the guides I knew routinely carried two sports up the river to fish its pools.

The first time I went up the Moose with two men aboard was one of the toughest days of my life. The heavy-laden canoe was sluggish, unresponsive. Fortunately, the river was fairly low so we were in no danger. But the current was strong, and I worked myself into a lather just reaching the first couple of pools to fish. Meanwhile, the old guides in our group, seemingly with little effort, disappeared around the bend. (Fortunately, the fishing that day was good. My sports were busy and happy catching salmon and never realized the strenuous effort I expended on their behalf.)

In time, my poling efforts improved and I expanded my range to the West Branch of the Penobscot and to the Allagash. One day I received a phone call from Harry Sanders, the latest in several generations of the Sanders family who operated the D. T. Sanders Store in Greenville. D. T. Sanders had been in operation for close to a century, starting by supplying the lumbering industry and later catering to the burgeoning Moosehead region tourist trade. If you wanted anything, from hardware to sporting goods to outdoors clothing and boots, to camping supplies and food, D. T. Sanders had it. It's no longer in business, but in its day it was the L.L. Bean of the North Woods. For many years, Sanders had outfitted canoe trips to the Allagash and St. John rivers and beyond, but now, Harry told me, he was in a bind. He was having difficulty finding guides. Most of the guides he had hired in the past were getting old and retiring, or preferred to stay closer to home. The younger guides were more interested in powerboats. Would I be willing to take an occasional party out on a canoe-camping trip? Of course. All I had to provide was my own canoe, paddles and pole, tent, and sleeping bag—everything else was furnished. Guiding trips out of Sanders was a joy.

The Templeton

Throughout this period, my White canoe served me well and faithfully. I was very pleased with its performance, assuming I already had the best. But the human heart is fickle, the head easily turned. One windy, blustery day several of us guides were paddling our sports on the lee side of Sand Bar Island on Moosehead. Away from the protected shoreline, the whitecaps were rolling three feet or more high, no place for a canoe. We paddled upwind, close inshore, protected by the trees. Near the north end of the island is a point that makes out to the east. We paddled out along the protected lee side of the point until we reached its end and encountered the force of the wind and waves, and then we'd swing the canoe downwind and let the wind carry us to the south end, and begin the circuit again. It was an effective tactic; evidently the action imparted to our trolled streamer flies by the bouncing waves enticed the salmon into striking. It was great sport.

I noticed, however, that one canoe, paddled by Rockwood guide Martin Munster, was more successful than the rest of ours. On each circuit, it would go out farther into the roaring rollers, where it seemed to dance and bobble jauntily. Its occupants were being kept busy catching and releasing fish. When we went ashore for the lunch break, I made it a point to look that canoe over. It was a patched-up, battle-scarred old veteran with some subtle differences from the Whites: It was deeper with a slightly more rounded bottom. I sat on a downed log next to Martin as we ate lunch and asked him about his canoe. "It's a Templeton," he informed me. "They used to be built right here in Rockwood. But old Mr. Templeton died years ago, and there's only a few of his canoes left."

I forgot about the incident until one day I learned that one of my neighbors (in that sparsely populated country, "neighbors" can live miles apart), Mert Comstock, had acquired a Templeton canoe mold and was building canoes in a shop on the shore of the Moose River. Oh, yes, I remembered! Martin Munster had one of these Templetons. Except he didn't, I later learned. Comstock's canoe mold came from a different Templeton, Fred. Munster's was an Arthur Templeton. Fred and Arthur were related—cousins, I believe—and both had been actively building canoes during the 1920s, '30s and '40s. Fred Templeton built his canoes in Greenville. Arthur's shop was on the Moose River, a couple of miles downstream from where Comstock set up for business.

Comstock's Fred Templeton was probably the best freight-and-lake canoe I've ever seen—deep, wide, flat-bottomed. Comstock also built a fifteen-foot version that proved very popular with pond-trout fishermen and trappers. He was soon so busy filling orders that he took on a partner, his son-in-law,

Fred Reckards. Their one concession to modernity was to cover their wooden canoes with fiberglass rather than canvas. It was tougher and could be left unpainted to reveal the beautiful wood-grained planking. Reckards continued to build Fred Templetons after Comstock died.

In time, I learned that another acquaintance had acquired an Arthur Templeton mold. Harold "Doc" Blanchard, a game biologist for the Maine Department of Inland Fisheries and Game, stationed in Greenville, began building Arthur Templetons part-time. By great good fortune, I stumbled upon one of them. My brother, Gene, had bought it from an acquaintance who had purchased it a couple of years before and seldom used it. The canoe was stored in his barn. Gene was only an occasional canoeist, and it wasn't too difficult to convince him to sell it to me. (Brand-new wood canoes at that time, the late fifties and early sixties, were selling for $10 a foot, or $200 for a twenty-foot canoe. Today, the same canoe would cost $3,000 to $4,000.)

My Doc Blanchard / Arthur Templeton was the best-handling, easiest-paddling canoe it's ever been my privilege to use. It had a slightly rounded bottom, and a bit of rise (called "rocker") at the bow and stern. It was fast and a joy to handle in quick water, where the ability to turn quickly is a tremendous advantage. It slid through the water like an otter. That canoe stayed with me for more than thirty years—longer than most marriages—long after I had left the guiding profession and moved on to other fields.

The Golden Years

In time, as I neared retirement age, I found I was using the
Blanchard/Templeton on fewer and fewer occasions. Most of
my canoeing was confined to smaller bodies of water near
home, and I usually used a smaller, lighter canoe. (Yes, I've
always been a multi-canoe person; no one canoe can fill all
bills. Over the years I've owned, sometimes simultaneously, a
fifteen-foot Grumman aluminum, which could be left at remote
trout ponds, and various Old Town fiberglass canoes.)

Finally my wife pointed out, quite sensibly—wives usually
are the level-headed ones when it comes to guys' attachment to
their toys—that I really didn't need a fleet of canoes anymore.
So gradually I began selling them off. First to go was the
Grumman, which I'd owned for at least forty years, and was
still as dry and in as good condition as the day I bought it from
Smith's Hardware Store in Jackman. It was a fine, serviceable,
stable, reliable canoe, but it was cold metal; it had no soul.
Next, the Old Town Discovery found a new home. Finally, it
was time to part with the beloved Blanchard/Templeton, which
I had recently had restored to pristine condition by Mike Biers
of Orrington. A doctor with a camp on Moosehead looked at
it and wanted it. I liked the fact that it was returning to its
Moosehead home and that the doctor planned to take it down
the Allagash with his son—better with him than sitting unused
with me. The canoe had a new lease on life.

Within a few weeks, I had a brand-new canoe: a lovely little lightweight Old Town Stillwater. It was fine for this old
geezer, light to load and unload, and easy to push around the
small trout ponds and bog holes I favor. For about a year,

things went along fine with the Stillwater. Then one day I made a terrible error. I went to a wooden canoe show.

The town of Millinocket, at the edge of Maine's North Woods, holds an annual Wooden Canoe Festival in August. My wife, Lorraine, and I decided to drive our RV over there just to look around and visit some friends. No way, at my age and retirement income, was I even thinking of buying a canoe. Well, when I spotted those lovely new canoes with their gleaming, varnished cedar planking and ribs, my heart began to flip-flop. It was a canoe-lover's paradise. But the price tags were sobering. These labor-intensive, artful creations started at $2,000 and went up from there. I tore myself away.

Later in the day we returned to the festival for a traditional bean-hole supper and it was then that I spotted a sixteen-foot, handmade beauty that hadn't been there earlier in the day. It wasn't new, but it obviously wasn't very old, and it was well-kept. Its price tag couldn't have been right, though; it was much too low. As we ate our beans under a colorful tent and visited with an old and dear friend, local guide and colorful character "Wiggy" Robinson, I couldn't shake the thought of it. After supper, I grabbed Wiggy's arm. "Come look at this and tell me if I'm crazy or imagining things!"

"Beautiful," said Wiggy when we reached the canoe. "Can that be the price?" I asked. "Sure looks like it." "If it is, I'm buying it," I exclaimed. Wiggy bent to look closer at the tag, which had the owner's name written on it. "Hey, I know this guy. He's a friend of my son's, and he builds his own canoes. Let's see if we can find him."

Within minutes we had confirmed the ownership and price and I had written the check. And that's how it happened that at an age beyond comprehension, I was in love again.

Trophy Salmon

One of the local Rockwood guides, Paul Edman, called me at Brassua Lake one day in the mid-fifties to see if I was up for a guiding job. The guide previously booked for the fishing trip had gone on a bender, Paul explained, and had to be replaced by someone who had a guide canoe and was willing to go camping for a week.

It was after the Labor Day rush and any opportunity in those early days of our fledgling sporting camp business was always welcome news to Anita and me. I lost no time in accepting the offer. Paul said he'd pick me and my canoe up the next morning and would fill me in on the details of the trip on the way.

It was early when we hit the road—in this case, the so-called "Northern Road," which heads north out of Rockwood to places like Pittston Farm, Seboomook Lake, Northeast Carry, and points north. At that time, it was the only such road penetrating into a wilderness area of several million acres.

Paul told me our destination only after swearing me to secrecy. ("If you tell anyone about this place, you're dead!") For several years, he and a small group of other guides had been bringing their sports to "the Foxhole," located near the mouth of a small brook some fourteen miles downstream from the put-in point at Northeast Carry on the West Branch of the Penobscot River. Landlocked salmon congregated at the Foxhole each fall. The fishing was fast and some of the salmon were giants. That's where we were headed now.

At the landing on the river, I met the other guides, our sports, who were from Pennsylvania, and the man hired on as the cook, Willie (not his real name). Willie, himself a guide, was getting on a bit in years, and those years were augmented by a life dedicated to Demon Rum. Wherever Willie was, a bottle was never far away. He seemed to exist in a perpetual alcoholic haze, never incapacitated, but always a little befuddled. He walked with a slight limp—when he was a young man he had been injured and partially crippled on a river drive—and his guiding days as far as paddling canoes, carrying packs, or hiking trail were long over. But Willie was still a fair-to-middling camp cook, capable of turning out rough woods fare that was suitable enough, with the exception of his fish chowder, which was superb.

After getting settled in camp, finishing supper, and spending the evening spinning yarns around the campfire, we turned in for the night. Soon our little clearing in the wilderness was resonating with the snores of a dozen tired guys in several tents. The next morning, after one of Willie's hearty breakfasts, we got into the canoes and hit the river.

The West Branch is a beautiful river. Despite decades of use as a highway for logs and pulpwood being floated down to the mills, its shores remain undeveloped and wild, and it's a great place to canoe and observe moose and other wildlife. It's the main tributary to Chesuncook Lake, and, as secretive guides had discovered, the lake's population of landlocked salmon favor it as a spawning area in the fall.

We were fishing mostly long, swift, deep runs, interrupted by riffles and moderate rapids. Our sports cast or trolled while we guides cruised them up and down in the canoes with a few stops at promising slicks or eddies. (This was before the river was restricted to fly-fishing only.) We weren't long getting into the salmon. The fishing was, in a word, fabulous.

Most of the sports had been to the Foxhole in previous years and knew what to expect, but, like me, my sport, Charley, was making his first visit. A banker by profession, he was rather short and a bit pudgy, and he had a ready smile and an affable nature—which was about to be put to the test. He was a fairly accomplished fly-caster, but he had never encountered fishing like this. I suggested he start by tying on a bucktail fly.

The first salmon hit that fly like a charging bull moose. Caught off guard, Charley nearly lost his rod overboard from the power of the strike. Then he jerked the rod up to set the hook and the fight was on. Charley was a taciturn type; he didn't scream and yell as some do when they first feel the power and explosiveness of a big, fighting landlocked, but his face split in a wide grin as he determinedly hung on. The salmon rolled at the surface, sounded into a deep hole behind a semi-submerged boulder, made a couple of reel-screeching runs across the river, and took a spectacular leap, sending spray flying and sparkling in the sunlight. Finally, spent, it came slowly to the side of the canoe. I slid the net under its body, being careful to keep the net bag before its nose so if it made a surge it would go in, not out. Then I lifted the net and the salmon was ours, nearly four pounds of silver lightning, its sides and back marked with little black crosses. Charley sat back and admired his prize. It was the biggest and fighting-est fish he had ever caught.

And so it went for the next couple of days. Charley was having the fishing time of his life. He managed to tie into several salmon each day. Meanwhile, the other sports in our party were doing well, too. Once or twice we had to move out of the way when someone nearby was fighting a fish. Sometimes we saw big fish just freely swirling or jumping clear of the water.

Paul Fournier/Courtesy Maine State Museum

The West Branch of the Penobscot River with Mount Katahdin in the background.

I think it was on the third day that Charley tied into his monster. We were working some eddies just below a ledge downstream from camp when the salmon struck. Something about the authority of that strike told me this was nothing usual. This was big. The fish tore off downstream, peeling off line so fast Charley couldn't grab the reel handle. The fly line instantly disappeared into the water, and the line backing was shrinking fast. I got on the paddle and started shoving our canoe down the river, trying to give Charley a chance to gain back some line. Then the salmon turned and headed upstream. I swung the canoe into a back-flowing eddy near shore, and paddled frantically to keep up with the surging fish. I don't know how long this to-and-fro tussle lasted; we'd lost all track of time. Unlike most salmon, this one didn't jump. A couple of times it came to the surface and swirled, and we caught a glimpse of its long, powerful body and broad side. This was a big fish—huge, in fact.

With his face grimly set, Charley made no noise, but simply put all of his concentration and effort into fighting that fish. He was doing a great job of keeping the rod pointed up, allowing it to bend and absorb the rushes and strains. I've seen rods, including my own, break on smaller fish than this. I watched with great anxiety. It was tempting to yell out advice, but Charley was handling it fine. I kept quiet, but my heart was in my throat: Was the leader strong enough? I had tied the fly on; was the knot slipping?

At long last, the fish was giving signs of tiring. The rushes and surges were shorter, less powerful. I eased the canoe into a quiet pocket below the ledge; and held it there, paddle ready to shove us out again if the fish took off. But its fight was over. Charley eased it close to the canoe, and we got our first good look. It looked as long as my canoe paddle. Its huge mouth gaped as it gulped in water to extract its oxygen. I could see the big hook (called a "kype") on its lower jaw, evidence this was a male. The fish was spent enough that netting it was routine. When I raised the net, the salmon's body, curved into the deep bag, was so long the nose touched the tail.

We did no more fishing that day. We immediately went back to camp, where the first order of business was to weigh the fish. It came in at an even nine pounds, the biggest salmon in camp by a substantial margin.

After the other fishermen repeatedly congratulated Charley and admired his fish, I began the meticulous job of preparing it for mounting, cutting a small slit in its side and extracting the innards. Then, using the established procedure for identifying a fish, Charley's name was written on a piece of paper and pushed into the salmon's mouth. The head guide had brought along several big insulated coolers loaded with ice blocks just for the purpose of keeping fish fresh, and we carefully, almost reverently, placed the salmon inside, being careful not to damage any of it scales.

That evening, the normally reserved Charley was almost ebullient at the campfire. The story of his great catch was repeated a number of times. Next day was more of the same. Charley's countenance was open and smiling. Our fishing was casual and relaxed. Mostly we cruised up and down, exploring the river and visiting with some of the other guys in our party. Charley described to me at great length the new room he'd recently had built at his home in Pennsylvania. It had a large fireplace and above it, a blank wall where his mounted giant salmon would hang in the place of honor. We went in for an early lunch, followed by Charley turning in for a nap. Before heading out on the river again, he went and admired his salmon resting on its bed of moss and ice in the cooler. Euphoria exuded from Charley's every pore. It was almost too good to be true.

The week was winding down. Charley caught several more "average" salmon—three- to four-pounders, what many anglers would kill for today. One late afternoon he even caught a handsome three-and-a-half-pound male brook trout in its brilliant fall breeding colors: bright red-to-orange belly, its red and black spots showing intensely in the brilliant autumn sunlight. After admiring it we eased the fly out of its lip and gently released it. One flip of its big square tail and it disappeared in the depths.

That evening before our last day of fishing Willie prepared his specialty: fish chowder. He outdid himself. It was delicious. He beamed under our plaudits—and that glow may not all have been due to Jim Beam.

The next morning I was on the riverbank getting the canoe ready when Charley walked toward me. I could see his look of consternation. He said, "Paul, where's my salmon?"

"It's in the cooler, where it's been all along," I responded. I didn't like his expression.

"No, it isn't!" he replied emphatically. "I just went and looked and it's not there!"

I led the way to the coolers. No way could that fish have disappeared. But it wasn't in the first cooler I looked into, nor was it in any of the others. There were plenty of other salmon in the coolers, beautiful, big salmon, an embarrassment of salmon, but there was no nine-pounder. This just couldn't be.

Beyond puzzled, Charley and I looked at each other. No one could have stolen it; there was no one else around but those in our party. And, there was no place else to keep such a prominent fish except in those ice coolers. Unless . . . naw, it couldn't be.

I walked over to the cook tent where Willie was puttering around, cleaning up after breakfast. Charley was on my heels.

"Hey, Willie, where'd you get the salmon for your chowder last night?"

Willie turned bleary eyes toward me. "Out of one of the coolers."

"Did you take the biggest one?"

"Yeah. I needed a big one to have enough to feed this gang!"

Willie never realized how close he came to being strangled on the spot.

Charley and I stood there, dumbfounded, but I think we both quickly realized there was no way to penetrate Willie's pickled brain. Shouts, curses, exhortations—none would make a difference. We turned away and left.

From walking on clouds one day, Charley was now the picture of utter despondency. His shoulders slumped, his head was down. He made sloppy casts with disinterest. And he had returned to his glum taciturnity.

The emotional dam broke that afternoon. We were just entering a sizable rapids downstream. Charley made a sloppy cast. His line wound around the spare rod he'd propped up in the bow of the canoe, wrapping itself into a nasty snarl. And Charley exploded. He stood up and began shouting every expletive he had ever heard and some I'd never heard. He ranted for several seconds, yanking at his rod, trying to loosen the tangled line.

We were just getting into the worst of the rapids. The canoe was rocking from side to side and water was slopping in over the gunwales.

I yelled at him: "Sit down, sit down, you're gonna dump us over!"

He finally regained his senses enough to plop back down in the bottom of the canoe. I maneuvered us through to a quiet eddy and began bailing out. We didn't say much to each other the remainder of the day.

In mid-afternoon all the canoes, by prearrangement, headed back to the campsite. Tomorrow morning we'd be breaking camp. We wanted to get some things packed and ready to load; tomorrow would be a full day getting home.

In late afternoon Charley came walking up to me with his fly rod in his hand. A bit surprised, I asked if he wanted to go out for a while before dark.

"No," he replied. "I just want to do a little casting from the shore."

The river was wide near the small gravel beach where we drew up our canoes. The current flowed past a little slower than most places. I wasn't aware of anyone catching a fish in this particular stretch all week, but I kept half an eye on Charley as I went about packing and lugging stuff down to the canoes.

Well, lightning struck for the second time that week. I heard a yell, and looked up just in time to see a big salmon— and I mean a BIG salmon—clear the water in a prodigious leap, then fall back with a splash. I dropped what I was carrying and raced for the riverbank, stopping only long enough to grab the net out of my canoe. Then, for the next fifteen minutes or so, I

stood behind Charley watching him battle that fish, occasionally offering a word of encouragement, but no advice. Charley
was playing him just right, keeping his rod tip fairly high to
absorb the shocks, releasing line when the fish ran, and hauling
it back in when he came closer, all the while maintaining a
judicious amount of pressure on the fish. This salmon, unlike
Charley's first big one, was a jumper, making several great leaps
and frothy splashes. Each time my heart was in my throat,
afraid the fly would pull out or the leader or rod would break.

By now, Charley was performing for an audience. Every
sport and guide had come down to the beach to watch the
action. The guides remained silent, save for a few low comments among themselves. There were a few shouts from
Charley's friends.

All its leaps and splashes must have helped to tire the big
fish out. It went to the bottom and sulked for a bit. Then its
runs were shorter and weaker. Charley, by now, was up to his
knees in the water. I stepped out and stood alongside him, net
at the ready. Then, as the fish was eased close to shore, I laid
the net down in the water where Charley could lead the fish
over it. A couple of times, the salmon came almost to the net,
but turned away and swam off a dozen yards or so. Charley
brought it back. Finally, Charley worked the salmon so its head
was directly aimed into the net. I lifted it, and we had him.

The gallery broke out in cheers and applause. The second
salmon, weighing within a few ounces of Charley's nine-
pounder, was its virtual mate—even to the kype on the lower
jaw.

Charley had pulled off a miracle: two giant salmon in one
week. And, he and Willie had provided us with an unforget-
table salmon chowder supper.

Bush Flying

Bush flying has appealed to me ever since, as a kid, I watched a pontoon-equipped Waco biplane of 1930s vintage take off and land on a pond near my home. For me, the sight of that plane lifting gracefully from the water and later skimming in for a landing was inspirational. I knew the people in the plane were using it to fly to remote, intriguing lakes and ponds in northern Maine. Within hours, or even minutes, they would reach places that otherwise required days of hard hiking or canoeing to reach, places where the trout and salmon were big and hungry and eager to be caught. Adding to my yearnings were the 1940s newsreels I watched at the Dreamland Theater in Livermore Falls: Famed aviator Charles Lindbergh and his wife, Anne Morrow Lindbergh, were flying all over the globe in their seaplanes, and I, too, wanted to fly like that, and to visit those same wild places.

My opportunity came while still a teenager, thanks to Ronnie Twitchell. Ronnie had followed his dream and built an airstrip from scratch. Not only did he clear the land and grade it smooth with a tractor, but he also hand-made cement blocks that he used to build an office and hangars, out of which he ran a flight school and an aircraft sales and service dealership. Ronnie gave me my first airplane ride, in a Piper J-3 Cub. After the first few thrilling minutes he had me place my feet on the

31

rudder pedals and a hand on the stick and I was *actually flying the plane*. His calm, reassuring voice from the front seat guided me through several gentle turns, climbs, and glides. When I could steal a glance outside, I saw the world as I'd never imagined it, a toy land of tiny cars and houses, cows in fields, and roads and lakes and rivers. I was hooked.

Ronnie and my brother, Felix, and I struck a deal. For $450 (in 1948 dollars, which would be about $4,300 today), Ronnie would sell us a shiny, canary-yellow, tandem two-seat Piper J-3 Cub. We made a down-payment, and Ronnie agreed to let us pay off the balance with no interest. We also agreed that on rare occasions when he needed the plane, he could use it and he'd apply credit toward our debt. And, he would teach me to fly it at the rate of $2.50 per hour of instruction time.

My flight training began immediately. It was January and there was virtually no heat inside that little fabric-covered airplane, not to mention the chill propeller wash blasting the cockpit. It was cold! We bundled up with heavy boots, jackets, long johns, gloves, and earmuffs. Ronnie had installed a set of skis on the Cub so we could continue flying no matter how deep the snow. (His field at the time had no paved runway. For the occasional wheel plane that showed up in the winter, a narrow strip was kept plowed along one edge of the field.) Ski flying requires a certain expertise. Planes with wheels use brakes to turn and stop on the ground. But because skis have no brakes, the pilot must use engine power, as well as the air rudder and sometimes the ailerons, in order to turn, especially when it's windy.

I made good progress. As we neared the grand total of eight hours of flying time, Ronnie and I set out for what we thought would be a half-hour of touch-and-go landings at the field in preparation for my first solo flight. As usual, things happen when least expected. The touch-and-go's were going routinely. We'd take off toward the east, climb to 600 feet, make a 90-degree turn to the left, climb to 800 feet, another 90 to left, then hold that altitude as we came downwind along the north side of the field parallel to the runway. With carburetor heat pulled on as we neared the end of the field (to prevent carburetor icing), the throttle would be pulled back to idle speed as we came directly opposite the spot on the field where I intended to touch down. With the plane in a glide, we'd make two 90-degree turns to line up with the landing strip. As the plane glided to within a few feet of the ground, the stick would be gradually eased back to "flare" the plane, holding it from touching until the speed was dissipated and the wings simply stopped holding the plane up and it settled onto the snow. Done properly, this results in the famous "three-point landing." (This was all in the days of "tail draggers," planes with two front wheels and one tail wheel. Tricycle-gear airplanes had yet to appear on the market.)

Ronnie and I had gone around the circuit several times, and I felt ready. My landings were spot-on. We made another takeoff and I felt sure this would be the last one before he turned me loose. I made the customary two turns to put us on the downwind leg, and we were at the midway point of that leg when the engine sputtered and quit dead.

My instant analysis of the situation looked pretty grim. The Cub, of course, had no starter; it required hand-propping. Difficult at 800 feet! I knew we didn't have enough altitude to reach either end of the runway. Landing across the field looked equally hopeless to my inexperienced eye: There didn't seem to be enough space between the tall trees at our edge of the field and the plowed-up snowbanks along the plowed section of runway. No other cleared space existed within reach of our gliding range. Visions of us crashing into the trees or smashing into the high snowbanks flashed through my mind. Without the accustomed roar of the engine, the plane was deadly quiet.

This all happened in a second or two. Ronnie later claimed that I said: "What do I do now?" All I remember is him shouting, "I'll take it!" I took my hands and feet off the controls and Ronnie instantly rolled the plane over into a steep, steep sideslip. A slideslip is a common maneuver used to lose altitude quickly without increasing airspeed, but Ronnie's sideslip was steeper than any sideslip I'd been taught in my training. We slid down from the sky as if on a greased pole. Ronnie leveled the plane off and we were on the snow, between the trees and the snowbank. After seeming to slide only a few feet along, the plane stopped. It was deathly still.

It seemed like we sat in that silent plane for a long, long time before Ronnie hopped out and reached for the Cub's gas "gauge"—a tall, thin piece of wire sticking up through the gas cap with essentially a cork stopper at the other end. The wire immediately dropped down with a clunk. We were out of gas.

How could that be? I always filled up the gas tank after flying to prevent condensation from forming inside the tank. I was positive I'd filled it up after the last time we'd flown a few days before. The tank held enough gas for more than three hours of flying; we'd been up less than an hour today. (Later I learned that an acquaintance had "borrowed" the plane without letting me know and had neglected to refill the tank.) During my preflight check I had made the mistake of failing to stick my finger in the tank to be dead certain it was full—just checking the gauge wasn't enough. We'd recently had a rainstorm followed by a cold snap, and evidently moisture had formed around the wire where it went through the cap and froze enough to hold it in place. Normally, you monitor this gauge while flying by noticing its bobbing up and down as it floats on the gas. When the top of the wire gets down to the cap, you know you only have a bit of reserve gas left and had better be handy to a landing place.

Ronnie and I trudged back to the office through the deep snow, found a gas can, filled it, and took it back to the plane. After a bit of priming and a few spins of the propeller, the engine roared to life. Ronnie asked, "You ready to go up again?" I must have looked a little reluctant. "It's like getting thrown off a horse," he insisted. "If you don't get right back on, you probably never will again." We climbed in, conducted our preflight check, and in a few minutes we were airborne again. We made several takeoffs and landings before calling it quits for the day.

A few days later, on a brilliant, clear, cold day in early February, Ronnie and I went around the traffic pattern a few times, and on the third landing he told me to pull up to the office. He got out of the plane, gave me a tap on the shoulder, and said, "Go ahead!"

The main difference I felt when I first took off alone was the lightness of the airplane. The little Cub fairly leapt off the ground without Ronnie's weight. The circuit around the traffic pattern was routine. Aware there was an audience watching, I concentrated on making the best landings possible. The lightened plane wanted to "float" longer than usual, but I managed three decent three-point landings before taxiing back to the office. Ronnie and several others greeted me with congratulatory handshakes and backslaps. Then Ronnie suggested: "Why don't you go up and play?"

The first solo was fantastic, but this was exhilarating. For the first time, alone, I could turn away from the home airfield and stretch my wings. I could try out all the maneuvers I'd been taught: climbs, turns, stalls, glides, spirals, slips. And I could simply gain some altitude and just float there, gazing out at the frozen world and enjoying this beautiful winter morning. Such a sense of freedom! It was euphoria such as I've seldom experienced since.

For the remainder of that snowy season, it was just a matter of getting to Twitchell's at every opportunity to build up flying time and learn and practice new techniques and maneuvers toward obtaining my private license. I recorded all my flights in my logbook, some solo, some dual time with Ronnie or his other instructor, Charlie Carrier. The book lists things like S-turns, "turns on and around pylons" (now called "turns on and around a point"), stalls, and more turns including 720s (two complete turns without gaining or losing altitude, etc.). All were designed to teach the student how wind affects a plane in flight and how to compensate for it, and how to be able to perform fairly intricate maneuvers without gaining or losing altitude. Meanwhile, I was also cramming with a stack of flight manuals and books on aeronautics, the dynamics of flight, the atmosphere, weather, and navigation.

Then it was time for my "solo cross-country," one of the eligibility requirements for the private pilot exam. The solo cross-country demonstrates the ability to fly over unfamiliar territory to several points without getting lost. To the neophyte flier, the Earth and its physical features can look very different than as seen from the ground. Hills look flatter, roads and bodies of water can be confusing, and distances are deceiving. When I made my solo cross-country, there were no "navigational aids" or means of communicating with the ground or anywhere else. Small planes like the Piper Cub, Taylorcraft, and Aeronca Champ had no electrical systems, no batteries, lights, or starters. The plane's engine ran off magnetos and didn't require external power. Two-way radios were virtually unheard of in light aircraft, and even if a pilot had use of one, only major airports were equipped to respond. Once aloft, you were strictly on your own.

Most small airports had no tower or any other way of contacting pilots. Instead, pilots were expected to follow certain traffic procedures so as not to surprise other pilots in the air or on the ground. If by chance (as rarely happened with me) a pilot of a small plane chose to land at a large airport serviced by a tower, the tower personnel communicated by flashing either a red light (Do Not Land) or green light (Cleared to Land). The pilot acknowledged receipt of the message by rocking his plane's wings. Crude and low-tech, but it worked.

As for instruments, there were only the absolute basics. A tachometer and oil pressure and temperature gauges made up the engine instruments. Flight instruments were an airspeed indicator, altimeter, and magnetic compass. All navigation was by visual flight rules: You looked at the ground and searched for features to match the map on your lap. You tried to judge the direction and force of the wind by watching for smoke or swaying tree branches, and, in summer, you'd use the size and direction of waves on a lake.

I made my first solo cross-country flight on March 31, a clear, bright day with light wind. I left Twitchell's at mid-forenoon. The first leg of my flight to the Heart of Maine

Flying Service airport outside Dexter was uneventful, even delightful. Visibility was unlimited, the air was smooth. I had marked the course on my map, and every landmark and checkpoint fell into place with regularity.

All went well until I sighted the Dexter airport and entered the traffic pattern at the prescribed 800 feet. Here was a problem. Dexter had a nice, paved runway that had been cleared of snow. The narrow grass area alongside the runway had also been plowed. I was on skis. There was a bit of snow left on the right side of the runway, but it didn't look like enough to safely land on. Besides, I couldn't tell if it was level, or a pushed-up snowbank. Someone came out of the hangar and waved his arms, but I couldn't decipher his meaning.

After circling the field a couple of times, I decided to land on still-frozen Lake Wassookeag a few miles away. From there, I walked the half-mile into town, found a phone, and called the airport. The airport manager, George Gerry, said he'd been the one waving his arms as I flew over, trying to indicate that there was, indeed, sufficient snow for landing on the right side of the runway. I returned to the Cub, took off, and in a few minutes landed on the patch of snow. There was enough snow to land on—just barely.

George helped me turn the plane around by hand so I could taxi back to the end of the runway in order to take off, and he signed my logbook, confirming my landing. When I told him I wanted to top off my tank for the remainder of my long flight, however, he couldn't help me—the airport was out of gas. I weighed my options: Either I could abort my plans and return to Twitchell's and try again another day, or press on ahead to my next planned stop at North Conway, New Hampshire, a flight of more than 100 miles. I had enough gas to reach North Conway with a bit of reserve left, so I thanked George for his help and climbed aboard. He propped the engine, and I was off on the next leg of my lone adventure.

The course to North Conway was southwest and I was bucking a headwind. The Cub cruised at about eighty mph, but my ground speed was somewhat slower than that. The engine droned sweetly on, time passed, and I watched that wire gas gauge in front of the windshield slowly drop. It was a bit agonizing. Should I call it quits and head back home while it was still possible? I kept going. In time I could judge from the contour of the hills ahead that I was getting close to North Conway. Finally, the airfield came into view. The gas gauge wire was still showing a bit above the cap and jiggling. I'd made it.

I'd been told this was a fairly active airport, but the field looked strangely quiet as I came in for a landing, and downright deserted as I taxied up to the gas pump in front of the hangar. Everything was locked up and there was not a soul in sight. I pondered my dilemma for a few minutes. I had to have someone sign my logbook to prove I had actually landed there or I'd have to repeat the whole trip. I still had one more card to play.

I walked over to a gas station across the road and talked over my problem with the lady proprietor. She didn't know why the airfield was deserted (and I never found out, either), but she did agree to sign my book, legally fulfilling that requirement. I considered buying enough gas to get me home from her, but she was selling Esso, and if I had to use other than 80-octane aviation gas, I needed Amoco, the closest auto gas to avgas. I thanked the gas lady, returned to the airplane, and took off.

My course now was east, back toward the home field, but I knew I'd never reach it. It was getting late; the shadows were long ahead of me, the sun sinking in the west behind the White Mountains. I didn't worry, though. Within a few minutes of leaving North Conway and gaining some altitude, I spotted ahead a long, narrow lake that I recognized as Long Lake, north of Sebago. At its north end was the town of Harrison. And in Harrison, I knew, there was an Amoco station.

In a short time I was throttling back and making a straight-in approach to the lake, no time for circling or traffic patterns now. The wire gas gauge had dropped to the top of the gas cap and had stopped jiggling. This was it; there was no going any farther. I landed on the lake ice, jumped out, and hurried as fast as I could to the town. The attendant at the Amoco station cheerfully filled a can with five gallons of gas, and even helped me carry it back onto the lake and out to the plane. He stood there smiling and waving the empty can as I opened the throttle and took off.

Dusk was falling, but I was only some twenty-five miles from home base. It was a beautiful evening. The air was smooth as silk as I flew in over Auburn's glittering lights and the traffic pattern for Twitchell's. Ronnie was still in his office when I taxied up and shut the engine down. He seemed surprised to see me back. All he said in his quiet, down-Maine way was, "I figured you must have had a problem and had to put down somewhere for the night." He signed my logbook, and the day—a rather full and tiring day—was finally over, my first cross-country solo complete.

After that, the road to my private ticket went smoothly. I took and passed both the written exam and the flight test on my first try. I was a pilot. And shortly thereafter, I became a full-fledged, certified seaplane pilot, too.

I kept my little Piper Cub, NC 98536, until 1950, when I enlisted in the Air Force after the U.S. went to war in North Korea. It was not a happy decision to give up my old friend, but it had to go. My new wife, Anita, and I were moving to Colorado, where I would serve as a technical instructor at Lowry Air Force Base in Denver.

When my four-year stint was over, Anita and I returned to Maine and within a month we became the proprietors of a modest, but promising (we hoped) set of sporting camps on Brassua Lake in the Moosehead region. The first couple of years were hectic and frenetic, and I had little free time to think about bush flying. Our property included several hundred feet of beautiful shoreline and I cleared off shorefront camping sites and opened a commercial campground, one of the first in Maine, to my knowledge. In the winter, we catered to ice fishermen, and I was constantly hauling firewood on my hand-drawn "moose" sled to the guests' cabins and to the string of ice-fishing shacks I rented out on the lake. I also took every guiding job I could find to augment our income.

The pull of flying was strong, however, and it eventually won out. I obtained my commercial pilot's license and started doing some work for Dick Folsom out of Greenville. Folsom's then was the busiest flying service in northern Maine.

Bush flying was seldom dull and always busy in the fifties and early sixties. Roads in the backcountry were rare, and most everything people consider essential to living in remote areas had to be flown in. The airplane became the taxi and the light truck, and pilots continued to find innovative, ingenious, and sometimes risky ways to use their craft and skills. It wasn't at all unusual to see any manner of material strapped to pontoons or jammed into cockpits with seemingly little regard for gross weight limits or aerodynamic effects on the already low-powered aircraft. Canoes were commonly hauled tied to the float struts, as were lumber, long pipes, sheet metal, etc. In hunting season, deer, as well as an occasional bear, were frequently hauled out strapped to the floats. Federal aviation inspectors would have been aghast had they been around to see how some pilots used their airplanes then.

On any given day as a bush pilot I might fly guests into or out of some remote sporting camp or to a place where they would tent out, like Lobster or Allagash lakes. I might have to fly a truck part or tractor part to a lumber camp, a mechanic to a river-driving towboat, or a technician to service someone's gas-powered refrigerator or cookstove. Often, it was supplies that filled the backseat of the plane, to be flown in to someone's remote camp.

One of the cargos I dreaded was flying gasoline to camps, where it was needed to fuel outboards, chain saws, and such. The rear seat of the Aeronca Sedan would be removed, and the entire rear compartment filled with as many five-gallon cans of gas as it would hold—making sure all covers were screwed on tight and that none leaked. I always took pains to fly as gently as possible and not jiggle those cans to set off a spark. A gasoline fire in that fabric plane would incinerate the plane—and me—in seconds.

A story circulated of a pilot from another company who, just as he attained flying speed and lifted off from the water, discovered a fire starting around the nozzle of one of the cans. Expecting the whole cargo to erupt any second, the pilot decided to jump out and take his chances in the water. As he pushed open the door, a blast of air entered the cockpit and snuffed out the flame. The grateful pilot reached back, screwed down that loose cap, and continued on his flight.

I recall one gas load I flew into a camp operated by one of the large landowning paper companies for use in entertaining company clients. A husband and wife had been hired by the company to run the place, the wife in charge of preparing meals for the guests, and the husband the all-around handyman. As I was getting ready to leave with the load, someone from the Folsom office handed me a paper bag to deliver to the husband, who'd called earlier to ask if some fishing tackle could be bought for him locally and sent in to him with the plane.

When I arrived at the camp, the husband, a cheery chap, met me at the dock. He helped me unload the gas, and he and I carried the cans up to a shed behind the main lodge. Along with the last can, I carried up the bag of fishing tackle. As we stood in the shack chatting, the guy's wife charged out from the kitchen and began searching frantically around the shack. She turned to me and began shrilly shouting: "What'd you bring him? What was in that bag? Did you bring him liquor? I've told the people at Folsom's to never bring him in any liquor! Don't you ever bring him in any liquor!"

I opened my mouth a couple of times to answer her, but she didn't give me a chance. The husband, meanwhile, was quietly looking over his fishing tackle and paying us no mind, as if he hadn't heard a word she said. I guess he'd heard it all before and was used to it. She was still haranguing him as I hurriedly walked back to the plane, untied, and shoved off.

On one flight, a passenger in my plane leaned forward and bit me on the arm. It was a Canada goose. We were flying it and some of its friends, both young and old, to the wild north as part of a project to relocate them from northeastern urban centers, where they, hooked on food handouts, had become pests. The biologists heading the project were well aware that the adults would eventually fly back to their city neighborhoods, but the strategy was that their goslings, who hadn't yet fledged, would imprint upon this new location and return in future springs to raise their own young.

To accommodate the birds, the backseat of my plane had been removed and the rear compartment was lined with plastic sheeting for easy cleanup afterward. Crates filled with geese and their goslings were stacked from floor to ceiling. At the destination the crates were taken out on the pontoon, opened, and the birds released in their new homes.

Was the relocation project successful? Anyone who has flown into Greenville on Moosehead Lake, or attended the annual International Seaplane Fly-in there and seen the several hundred geese flying in and out in formation has seen part of the result. Similar sights are now found in many parts of the state. Some people, whose lawns and beaches have been befouled, think it has worked too well.

Bush flying, while amazing, can be tough. There's always the weather to contend with. When the clouds drop low, pilots often find themselves "scud running," picking their way from pond to river to lake, relying on their experience and knowledge of the country to avoid hills or mountains. Sometimes they have to drop down onto a lake and wait out the weather. Bush pilots usually have fishing parties camped out at remote lakes and ponds who have been told they'd be picked up on a certain day, at a certain time. When the weather goes marginal, pilots are always torn: Do those people have enough food? Are they adequately protected from the elements? Should I take a chance and try to go in and get them out? Then there's always the worst-case scenario, a crash in the wilderness.

When it became necessary for Anita and me to sell our camp business and move on with our lives, it also meant, for me, leaving the world of commercial bush flying. It had been exciting, fun, and sometimes frightening, but I knew deep down I was a "fair-weather" pilot. What top-notch bush pilots shrug off as just a day's work was too stressful for most ordinary mortals, me included.

The final, deciding factor for me, though, was learning that Ronnie Twitchell—my mentor, my good friend, the man who had made flying possible for me—was killed in a plane crash. Ronnie, the most conscientious, cautious, natural pilot I'd ever known, had, unbelievably, incredibly been killed not on some risky flight in the wilds, but at the end of his own runway. I've heard theories as to what caused the crash, but I wasn't there and do not care to comment or speculate. That Ronnie Twitchell could die in a simple accident on his home field was devastating.

I continued to own and fly airplanes for business and for my own pleasure, but the pressing demands of commercial bush flying were now behind me. I was a bush pilot for a relatively short period, but it was a precious and memorable time. It is a part of my life that I look back upon with fondness and a bit of pride.

Versions of this chapter first appeared in the Aircraft Owners and Pilots Association's *AOPA Pilot* magazine and in the Seaplane Pilots Association's *Water Flying* magazine.

Rampaging Black Bears

Some years ago a fisherman camped alone at one of my favorite sites, "The Eight-Holer," on the shore of the West Branch of the Penobscot River north of Millinocket. (Back in the lumber-driving days this was the location of a major river-drivers' camp featuring an outhouse with eight holes.) After a successful day of fishing, he cleaned his catch and went to bed. In the middle of the night he was awakened to a black bear sniffing and pawing at his tent. Suddenly, the bear pulled the tent down on top of the fisherman and began walking over him, "kneading and feeling me through the tent cloth." Then the bear started to chew on the man's legs. The poor guy managed to drag himself out from under the tangle of bear, tent, and sleeping bag and ran to a tree, which he climbed. Thank goodness for him, the bear—perhaps finally realizing the fisherman was a human and not a fish—didn't climb it, too. Bears are excellent climbers. The man stayed in the tree until daylight, when, satisfying himself the bear was no longer around, he climbed down and sought help. He was taken to the hospital in Millinocket where he was treated for deep puncture wounds in his thighs.

Fortunately, even though Maine has one of the higher bear populations among the Lower Forty-Eight, such incidents have remained rare.

In the fifties, when I first encountered them, bears were considered vermin and always had been. Many states, including Maine, paid a bounty for each bear killed. Unlike today, virtually everyone who went into the woods then carried a gun, and any bear encountered was a dead one, so bear populations were kept in check. Today, bears are no longer considered varmints, but prey. The Maine bear harvest in the fall of 2010 was 3,062, comparable to previous years, according to Randy Cross, a wildlife biologist and leader of the Maine Bear Project. With a population conservatively estimated at 23,000, this is considered below the harvest objective of 3,500 desired to stabilize the state's bear population. The economic value of bear hunting in Maine is estimated at $50 million, Cross says, and since a large percentage of Maine bear hunters come from other states, this means a substantial influx of money into the state.

When I operated the camp on Brassua Lake, bears were occasional visitors, and we didn't have to wander far into the woods to run into bear signs. Not infrequently, camp guests driving along our access roads saw bears. By hauling off trash frequently, keeping the campsites clean, and advising campers to keep their food stored away, we avoided most serious conflicts. Others weren't so lucky.

Driving along a woods road north of Greenville one day, I was monitoring the two-way radio tuned to the frequency used by game wardens and biologists. Here's what I heard:

"2-2-2-5 to 2-2-2-7, I just came by your camp [Lily Bay warden camp]. I hate to tell ya, but a bear's been in there and raised hell. He broke in through the back window, and he trashed it pretty bad. Tore and messed up your sleeping bag, bit through all the food cans, and hauled off your cooler. I found [the cooler] up in the woods. He ate everything, even ate your hot dogs."

2-2-2-7 came back on the radio: "Even my hot dogs?" His voice was almost a plaintive wail.

I was near the scene of the crime so I drove over to the camp and looked around. There were clear tracks on the wall where the bear had clawed its way up, and sure enough, the window was broken. As I looked over the damage, the warden who first spotted the mess, Roger Guay, arrived towing a live-bear trap—actually a piece of modified metal road culvert on trailer wheels. Roger baited and set the trap. The next day he called to tell me they had trapped the bear and hauled it far north to, hopefully, a new home away from enticing humans.

Lumber camps used to draw bears from miles around. Being situated far back in the woods, and invariably having lots of foodstuffs on hand and a refuse dump close by, the camps were virtual bear magnets. In the days before chain saws, it was common practice to spike sections of old crosscut saw blades to cabin windows in hopes of discouraging bruins. If bears smelled something edible inside an empty camp, though, they could be counted on to find a way in. I remember one cabin on Lower Richardson Lake where a bear not only ripped off the saw blades, but it also tore off nearly an entire wall—shingles, board sheathing, studding—to gain entrance and ransack the place. Every lumber camp had its wealth of bear stories.

Bob Eastman, a guide, trapper, camp operator, and timber cruiser, told me one of the better bear stories I've heard. Bob was on a crew of timber cruisers (surveyors) who had set up headquarters at an abandoned lumber camp on Baker Lake near the headwater of the St. John River. The camp served the cruisers just fine. The only thing unusual about it was the cabin

Black bears are attracted by anything that smells in the least bit edible.

they were using as a cookshack. It had a long, overhanging second story held up by a lone post; there used to be other supporting posts, but they had fallen down. The cook had taken over the second story as a combination supply room / bedroom.

A very large and extremely wily bear was bothering the camp nightly. Although the men stayed up several nights in an attempt to shoot it, the bear had so far managed to elude them. With the bear's predations becoming more brazen, one of the men got a flash of inspiration. He found an empty wooden barrel that once contained salt pork (a lumber-camp staple), and used boards and spikes to narrow the head of it, leaving just enough space in the middle for the bear to get its head in, but making it difficult to get it out. He then poured a half-gallon of molasses into the barrel. Finally, he hitched a long, tough logging chain to it and wrapped the other end around the cookhouse post.

Long past midnight one night, with the men sleeping the sleep of the exhausted, the bear returned. He stuck his head into the barrel to lap up the tasty molasses, but when he tried to pull it out, he was stuck. Stuck like a skunk with its head caught in a jar. One can picture him shaking it violently to no avail and giving his body a shake of annoyance. Then, letting out a huge bawl of rage, he jumped for the woods, the barrel tenaciously hanging on. Behind him the chain slithered out and came taut with a sharp jerk.

Imagine, for a moment, the plight of the poor cook: Rudely awakened by the bear's loud bawl, in the next instant he heard the post splinter and break. The building tilted crazily for a second and then crashed to the ground, the cook deluged under an avalanche of pots, pans, bags of potatoes, canned goods, and assorted condiments!

Today the nuisance bear is more likely to be live-trapped, tranquilized, and relocated to some—supposedly—remote location. But bears don't always take kindly to relocation. They can, and will, travel considerable distances to return to their favored home ground. Take, for instance, the case of a bear that had been captured in Warren as a nuisance after it raided several beehives used for pollinating a blueberry crop. That bear was transported to T32 MD, an unorganized township in eastern Maine, and dropped off. Later it was killed by a hunter. Where? Back in Warren. This bear traveled over seventy-five miles from the time it was released in T32 MD to the town of

Warren. "We were able to identify it by the registration number that had been tattooed on the inside of its lip. Bears have been known to travel over a hundred miles after being relocated, and this one was no exception," said Allen Starr, a wildlife biologist with the Maine Department of Inland Fisheries and Wildlife.

Bears become a nuisance for a number of reasons, not the least of which is their voracious appetites. A northern bear is driven by an irrepressible need to fatten its body during the brief summer in preparation for the five to seven winter months it will spend in its den. When wild food becomes scarce, the opportunistic bear begins raiding homes, cabins, farms, and campsites. Furthermore, encroaching humans, urban sprawl, and beech tree afflictions (beech trees are a primary food source for bears) have displaced some bears and caused them to become even more of a nuisance.

Still, the average wild black bear is a shy, retiring creature. Given a choice, it prefers to shun humans, remaining deep in its native woods, minding its own business. The average wild black bear occasionally encountered in the woods is no more dangerous to humans than are rabbits or squirrels. With their instinctive and deep-rooted fear of man and their superior senses of scent and hearing, they become aware of the approach of a relatively clumsy human and fade away into the woods long before our arrival, leaving only tracks to attest they are around.

There is one exception: the female with cubs. She can be a formidable protector of her young, and the Maine woods are rampant with tales of woodsmen escaping from enraged sows by the skin of their teeth. (Some may even have been true!)

My own story comes from the time in the 1950s when I was a bush pilot for Folsom's Air Service in Greenville. I had flown a mechanic to Chesuncook Lake so he could fix a tugboat used by log-driving crews to haul log booms across the lake. Lunch was served at the crews' camp several miles up the West Branch of the Penobscot River, and we took a boat to get there. After lunch, the tug captain and I decided to walk back to the plane and boat, using a trail through the woods. We struck out, with me leading the way.

We'd been walking about ten minutes when, as I stepped around a bend, I spotted the tail end of a bear cub scooting around the next turn.

Amused, I turned to my companion. "Did you see that?"

"No. What was it?"

"A little bear cub just—" I started.

"A cub!" he exclaimed, eyes growing wild. "The old lady must be around. Let's get the hell out of here!"

Just then the mother came charging around that next bend, headed toward us, two cubs at her heels. She stopped and glared at us, teeth bared and hackles bristling. She looked huge! She began hissing and popping her gleaming, yellowish teeth. Have you ever heard a bear popping its teeth? It's an attention grabber.

This bear was bluffing. After glaring us down, she turned and led her cubs back into the thick forest. But she gave me my own bear story, nonetheless.

Giant Wild Trout

It was a gathering of brook trout such as I'd never seen before. They were crowded by the dozens into the shallow pools of Misery Stream. Most, I guessed, were in the three- to four- pound class, but there were several considerably larger—maybe five to six pounds, or even more. (I know, it's easy to exaggerate fish sizes when you're excited!) In some places the stream was so shallow their dorsal fins and backs were out of water. At times the stream would suddenly explode with fish activity into a flurry of white foam.

It was a late October day in the fifties. These trout were here, seven or eight miles upstream from their home, Brassua Lake, to spawn.

Brook trout are particular in selecting a habitat, especially spawning grounds. For one thing, it is probably the least tolerant of all fishes to polluted or silted waters. For another it is truly a cold-water fish, seldom found in waters warmer than 60 to 65 degrees and generally preferring it colder. The ideal egg-incubation temperature is 40 degrees, and for its spawning grounds, the trout chooses a stretch of streambed that is fed by underground springs so it gets a constant supply of cold, clean water. Apparently, these pools on Misery Stream were just right.

I returned to this spot several times in subsequent days to watch the dozens of big, beautiful trout in their annual ritual, and one day while scouting the stream between Brassua and the spawning grounds, I found out how difficult it was for these trout to get there. Several miles upstream from the lake was a ledge, which, judging by the old, rotting timbers and cribwork there, had been at one time the site of a small dam used for log-driving. It was several feet high and created a formidable waterfall obstacle to the upstream-migrating trout. The only way over was to jump. And jump they did.

I spent many hours sitting on the bank watching the trout fighting to get over the water pouring down over the ledge. They would leap repeatedly, resting and gathering strength in the deep pool below the ledge before trying again. Only occasionally did I see one make it over, and then only at a certain spot where a crack in the ledge momentarily slowed the force of rushing water. Most had to try over and over. They didn't seem capable of calculating their leaps; some hit the bare ledge, and, when I went close, a couple actually struck my legs. They seemed oblivious to everything but the overpowering urge to get over the ledge and reach the spawning area.

While in the shallow stream, the trout were vulnerable to predation, as evidence at several locations showed. I saw a few fish with stab-like wounds in their backs, likely the victims of great blue herons that had killed them but then found them too big to swallow. I also saw fresh fins and trout eggs on the stream bank where some animal—mink, otter, possibly even a foraging bear—had stopped to dine.

Back at the spawning beds, some of the larger males sported kypes, and all of the males' bellies and fins were alive with color, ranging from glowing orange to nearly blood-red.

The roe-heavy females, dull in comparison with the flamboy-ant males, had distended, rounded conformations.

The trout stay on the beds for several days to a week or more, and their presence is marked by considerable thrashing and splashing. The males, now aggressively vying for the females' attentions, engage in many battles marked by nipping, shoving, and lightning-fast chases up- and downstream. Males have been seen to lock jaws and roll over and over down a long stretch of rapids.

Seemingly unmindful to this violence staged for her bene-fit, the female critically selects a suitable site and busies herself in preparing the "redd," or nest. Lying on her side near the bot-tom of the stream, she violently flaps her blunt, powerful tail up and down. Currents generated by the action loosen bottom material and wash it downstream. Alternately flapping and rest-ing, she remains at the task until the nest's dimensions suit her. Generally it's from four to twelve inches deep and one or two feet in diameter, depending to some extent on her size. When the nest is ready, the female slowly swims in over it and remains there nearly motionless, while one or sometimes two males move next to her, vibrating their bodies and pressing against her sides. Eggs and milt (sperm) are released simultane-ously. Fertilization takes place as they drop into the nest and are mixed by currents. The female then immediately moves upstream and loosens some bottom material, which is carried downstream and covers the fertilized eggs in the nest.

In a few days the run is over for the season and the trout are exhausted from their energy-sapping ordeal. For weeks, they've battled frothing white rapids, leapt over waterfalls, and evaded predators. Now they drop back downstream into the lake, where, under the protective mantle of ice, they'll spend a relatively quiet winter, feeding and slowly regaining their strength. It takes many weeks to recuperate, and many of the fish do not show their characteristic vitality until late winter or early spring.

Meanwhile, water percolating through the loose bottom gravel of the spawning beds keeps the fertilized eggs moist and supplied with oxygen during the incubation period, which varies with the water temperatures. (At 40 degrees, it takes about ninety days.) After hatching, the young trout—now known as sac fry or prolarvae—remain in the nest for many more weeks, taking nourishment from the attached yolk sac until it is absorbed. At that point they wriggle up through the gravel and emerge into the stream. Advanced fry remain in the stream for one to three years. During their early life, they feed primarily on immature aquatic insects and other minute animal life, later graduating to larger insects and finally to other fish. Growth rate varies considerably, depending on the individual stream's productivity, but generally trout reach the legal limit of six to eight inches in their second year.

A year after I first watched the leaping trout on Misery Stream, I returned to the falls, this time armed with movie and still cameras. It was an interesting challenge, trying to catch these fish in midair. There was no warning—when they jumped, it took a split-second reaction to snap the camera and catch them. For the stills, I used an advanced Nikon camera with fast shutter speed and fast lenses. I missed plenty and wasted a lot of film, but I managed to capture a fair number of leaping trout. It turned out these were extremely rare; there is an abundance of photographs of jumping salmon, but not of sizable trout.

A trout leaps high in an attempt to get over a ledge on Misery Stream on its way to a spawning ground.

Flushed with this success, I planned to be there the next year to get more such shots. But it wasn't to be. During the winter, a large pulpwood-cutting operation had moved into the Misery Stream valley. A big lumber camp, housing dozens of woodcutters, was set up by the streambed, very close, in fact, to the spawning beds. This was in the days when wood was still being moved down to the mills by river drives. By late winter, bulldozers were hauling trailer loads of pulpwood to the banks of Misery Stream. The stream banks themselves were bulldozed flat; trees and brush were shoved back to make room for stacking the wood. Long rows of piled-up, four-foot pulpwood were stacked up on both sides of the stream for miles. The streambed between the rows was bulldozed flat and smooth—it actually became the roadbed for the tractor-drawn wood trailers. When spring arrived, the bulldozers were again brought into play, this time to push and shove the stacks into the swollen stream. When a logjam occurred, the dozers shoved the wood down the stream.

When the drive was finished, the stream's trout habitat was no more. No longer were there pools and rocks where water was deep enough for trout to hide and rest. No longer were there trees or brush to provide cooling shade for the young trout fry. To this day, a half-century later, no big trout have ever again been seen jumping at the falls. Despite frequent checks, Department of Fish and Wildlife monitors have not documented any spawning in Misery Stream over the years, nor have I seen any myself. As if this weren't tragic enough, perch were introduced into the waterway—disastrous to the vulnerable trout.

Unfortunately, this is only one among many similar horror stories that arose during an environmentally insensitive period in the state. It wasn't until 1976, when public outrage forced the Maine Legislature to face the issue it had ignored for decades, that river driving was ended by law. It was replaced, however, by a network of thousands of miles of graveled roads, which created problems of their own by releasing silt and gravel into streams and providing easy access to previously iso-lated waters.

Can anything be done to restore the Misery Stream spawn-ing ground and others that have been destroyed? It is easy to realize the enormity of the task when one considers that such a large state as Maine has only seven regional biologists, each with only two assistants, and each managing a region roughly the size of Connecticut. It took years to do the damage, and it will take many more years—along with manpower, equipment, and vast amounts of money, all of which are unavailable now and in the foreseeable future—to undo it all.

Fishing biologist Forrest Bonney has made some progress on one stream, however. He has built several "sediment traps" on Cupsuptic, a tributary of Mooselookmeguntic Lake in western Maine. The traps, which basically are logs laid across the streambed with boulders piled on top of them, are low enough to allow the passage of trout up and down the stream, but they trap the silt and gravel. He is working on a similar project on nearby South Inlet Bog Stream, a major spawning tributary to Rangeley Lake.

Bonney says several waters in his region are already producing nice-sized fish, if not in large numbers. Mooselookmeguntic Lake recently began producing some good spring trout fishing, including a six-pounder—something not seen in years. Rangeley, which over the years had lost all its native wild trout, is responding well to an initial stocking of 500 Kennebago-strain brookies, with some nice catches during the past couple of seasons. The trend is encouraging.

It's unlikely Maine will ever again capture the glories of a century or even fifty years ago, but, thanks to dedicated and farseeing people like Forrest Bonney and his colleagues, the state's future trout fishing should be considerably better than today's.

A version of this chapter first appeared in *Natural History* magazine.

DIFW Days

In the fall of 1980 I received a call from Tom Shoener, who had been recently promoted to the position of director of public information and education at the Department of Inland Fisheries and Wildlife. He offered me a job.

This was a tough period for the department—and specifically for Tom's division. I had already been doing a fair amount of contract work for them, producing television news stories and writing articles for the department-produced magazine, *Maine Fish & Wildlife*, so I was aware of some of the department's operations and its problems.

The job he offered was a newly created position labeled "media coordinator." I would pretty much have a free hand in developing the nature of the job, but there were caveats. Tom confided that the department's relations with the media were either almost nonexistent or adversarial. Bad blood had developed between members of the press and some members of the department, notably some biologists and wardens who had refused to provide information or acted arrogantly. Not a wise move to cross the media; they always have the last word, and control what the public reads or sees on TV. Also, Tom told me, rifts had developed within the agency. In particular, the warden service branch had become disillusioned (to put it kindly) with the information and education division.

Compounding the situation was that this was in the wake of the Watergate scandal. Suddenly, almost anything to do with government, at about every level, was at best suspect if not downright scandalous or felonious. (So, what's changed?) And there was more than a little muckraking journalism out there. There's the cliché in media circles of the zealous journalist working on a sensational story when new, solid information emerges. His response: "Don't confuse me with the facts—I got too good a story goin' here!"

This was the firestorm I was invited to step into.

Why would I, at age fifty, even consider accepting such a potentially incendiary position? There were several factors at work. I was just into my tenth year of running my small film production company. There had been good times and bad times. I'd lucked out and connected with a number of good clients. I'd had a lot of fun along the way, including travels to many parts of the country and the world. While I'd never struck it rich, neither had I gone into debt, and I had a comfortable lifestyle filled with enriching experiences while pretty much being my own boss and calling my own shots.

But I could see problems on the horizon that were likely to interfere with this idyllic life. First was age: How could I, slipping past middle age and seeing retirement age creeping toward me, expect to continue such an insecure, physically demanding lifestyle far into the future? A serious illness or accident would immediately wipe out my primary source of income. Then, things were not looking too rosy in the small end of the film production field. Film production as I practiced it in my one-man-band operation was very labor-intensive, although relatively inexpensive. The times, they were a-changing, however. First of all, Eastman Kodak, the major supplier of 16-mm motion picture film, was changing the ball game. In the late seventies, Kodak came out with new emulsions that completely revolutionized and improved the quality of the 16-mm film image. The change came at a price, not only in the higher cost of film but in production costs as well. The film could only be handled for editing in "clean-room" environments, free of dust. Postproduction, much of which I had handled personally, now had to be outsourced to specially equipped facilities. Costs shot up exponentially.

The other ominous development was the emergence of that new kid on the block: video production. Every few months newer, better, mysterious electronic boxes and cameras were coming out, mostly from Japan. Video producers were competing with us film producers for production contracts, and they were garnering more and more of them. The handwriting was on the wall, and there was no way that I, at my age, could consider going into this new, complex medium. (Though eventually I did.)

And so, with all factors considered, I accepted Tom's offer. I leapt into the firestorm.

In accepting the job I thought, perhaps naively, that I had a few things in my favor. After several decades of guiding, flying, camping, fishing, hunting, and filming, I was more familiar with the state and its people than many of the department staff. I'd written for various media and provided news film and footage to television stations and producers, including NBC, CBS, and ABC, so I already had many contacts that could be called upon to disseminate the department's stories. Having been on contract to the department, I had already met and worked with various wardens and biologists, including some of those who were now in disfavor with the working press. Finally, having at one time worked as a newspaper reporter and editor, I knew what reporters needed and the demands and deadlines they worked under.

And so I was launched on the final chapter of my checkered career, laying out this dictum to my employers, media representatives, and myself: I would never knowingly release false or misleading information. I never varied from that. It was the only way to establish and maintain trust with the press and the public.

One of the first things I did was get out of the headquarters in Augusta and get out to the boonies, to the regional offices scattered around the state, to meet with the troops and to begin to heal sore wounds. I met with as many wardens, biologists, and technicians as possible. Some expressed amazement that anyone would bother to leave the comfy confines of an Augusta office to actually come out and see what they were doing. This worked out on several levels. Not only did it establish a rapport, but it also brought me up-to-date on what people were doing in research, management, and protection of the state's wildlife resources. It also provided me with grist for the news releases I began churning out to the media and public.

The truth of the matter is that the department was a gold mine of great stories about wildlife and its protection and management. These were just the type of stories I loved to work on—actually, in essence, an extension of the type of stories I had written for magazines, newspapers, and television. I was able to mine this mother lode for the rest of my career. Many times during the years at DIFW I was accused jokingly (I think) of being "paid to play." I never denied it. It was right up my alley. Almost every day was pure joy. How many people can say that about their jobs?

But my job had its downside, too: reporting about the people who got into trouble while in the Maine woods and on its waters—people who got shot, drowned, got lost. At times I had so many of these tragedies to report that many people I met thought that was all I did. It was the newsworthy, most visible part of my job, but in reality, only a small part of it.

The most frequent of the tragedies was drownings, usually beginning right after ice-out in the spring, one of the more productive fishing times of the year, when trout and salmon are at the surface and feeding voraciously on spawning smelts. It's hard for many anglers to resist that call even when weather conditions should keep them ashore. It's a time when the water temperature is only a few degrees above freezing, and when weather can quickly turn nasty with storms and strong winds. Anyone falling in has only a few minutes of survival time under these conditions.

The typical situation goes like this: A middle-aged guy goes fishing alone. His boat is found empty, drifting, or washed against the shore. The engine control is set at trolling speed, the tank run dry of gas. Fishing tackle is all in place, trolling rods in their holders. A partially consumed six-pack of beer is in the boat.

Searching for the body is made difficult under such conditions: Where to start looking? Where had he been when he fell overboard? On big lakes this can be anywhere from hundreds of yards to several miles away. Occasionally, some other fisherman says: "Oh, yeah. I saw him trolling off such-and-such point." But usually the Warden Service Search and Rescue team has to rely on experience and savvy to narrow down the

67

likeliest search area by taking into account wind speed and direction to determine the starting point. Then they set out buoys and begin a grid search pattern—towing two wet-suited and SCUBA-equipped divers on ropes behind a boat. Given decently clear water conditions, these guys are remarkably successful at recovering the body, even if it might take several days.

Of those drowning victims found, a surprising number have a common denominator: Their flies are open. The theory? The guy was out there fishing alone, wearing warm, bulky clothing to ward off the cold, and drinking his beer. In time, with all that beer and cold air, his bladder asks for relief. He's alone, he doesn't want to take time out from fishing to go ashore, and he forgot to bring his empty tomato can. So he stands up at the edge of the boat. Somehow—not too difficult to imagine, considering his alcohol intake, unstable footing, and likely cold-stiffened joints—he teeters and falls overboard. If he hasn't clipped on the dead-man lanyard that would cut the motor—how many do?—the boat continues trolling away from him as he struggles in his bulky clothes and heavy cold-weather boots for the final couple of minutes of his life. If he'd been wearing his personal flotation device—again, how many do?—it might have kept him afloat and alive for at least a short while, possibly long enough to reach the shore if not too far out.

It never failed to surprise me back then how so many people take unnecessary, even foolish, risks on the water. They venture out into the wildest conditions in tiny boats and canoes totally unsuited to the task. It seemed the less the experience, the greater the chances they took. When I first started guiding in canoe country, the guides' choice of craft was

invariably the twenty-foot canoe. They wouldn't dream of setting out on big water in anything less. (The exception: small
lightweight canoes used for portaging into small trout ponds,
where they were protected from winds and never far from
shore.) And, whenever possible, the guides stayed reasonably
close to the shoreline. Only rarely would they venture to cross
large, open expanses of unprotected water. They were only too
aware that winds around big water can spring up fast and unexpectedly. Given a choice, they'd take the long way around,
hugging the shore. That's how they lived to become old, experienced guides. Yet, how many times have I seen raw neo-
phytes get into tiny watercrafts and set out blithely into
conditions that kept even sizable craft tied to their docks? A
couple of other dangerous phenomena I've observed from inexperienced boaters and canoeists: Almost invariably, they head
out toward the middle of the biggest water, and if they're leaving from a protected lee shore, they always head downwind, or
in a river, downstream, with no thought of the difficulty they
will face bucking the wind or current to come back. Often,
they have to be rescued.

On a wild day at Brassua Lake with the wind gusting to
twenty- to twenty-five miles per hour and big whitecap waves
rolling down the lake, all our boats were safely hauled ashore.
No one dreamed of going out. I was at the dock when to my
astonishment, I saw a flotilla of a half-dozen canoes emerge
from the outlet of Little Brassua some five miles uplake. It was
obviously one of the many canoe-camping youth groups taking
the Moose River trip from Jackman to Moosehead. On the
map that trip looks like a piece of cake, but in reality it can
entail some moderate whitewater rapids, depending on water
levels, and some big open water.

I trained my binoculars on the canoes and again was aston-
ished to see that instead of hugging the lee western shoreline
where they'd be protected from the wind and waves, they
headed right out to the middle and were caught in the wind,
which drove them straight down the middle. The farther down
the lake they came, the stronger the wind-sweep and the bigger and angrier the waves. And they were coming fast. Their
canoes were heavily laden with two or three persons in each
plus their camping equipment and supplies. Once caught in
that maelstrom, there was no turning. Any attempt to turn
sideways would have immediately swamped them. They were
getting the ride of their lives—nearly the last ride of their
lives.

Within minutes they were approaching my small dock, the
only safe landing place on that entire shore. Beyond the dock
the shore was all rock ledge and dri-ki. I grabbed a long pick-
pole (a long wooden pole with a metal spike at the end used
by river drivers) and stood at the end of the dock. As the first
canoe came by I held the pole out at arm's length. One of the
kids grabbed it and I braced my feet and swung the canoe into
the quiet water on the lee side of the dock. One after another I
grabbed each canoe and swung them in until all six were safe.
Some of the kids got out and hugged and kissed the ground. A
couple of young girls vomited. The kids, from a youth camp in
southern Maine, spent the rest of the afternoon drying their
clothing and gear in the wind and sun and recuperating. Later,
toward evening, the wind died and they were able to continue
their trip to the Lower Moose River and their destination,
Moosehead Lake. They had come mighty close to never making it. I hope they realized their folly and learned a vital lesson
in survival.

People get into trouble on Maine waters year round, but next to summer, the busiest season for drownings is winter. Children, especially, find fresh-frozen pond or river ice irresistible, and all too often break through. I particularly recall an incident on the Saco River when two young brothers fell through and drowned. I was there when the warden divers, swimming among the ice blocks, retrieved the two little towheaded forms. The parents' grief was beyond description.

Most of the time, when people break through the ice, it's because they're riding a vehicle—snowmobile, car, or truck—where they shouldn't be. It doesn't matter how cold the air is—it could be 25- or 30-below zero—it's still possible to have thin or weak ice. This is a message we put out repeatedly through the news media over and over and over. Moving water is always above the freezing point. Water moves around points, through narrows, and particularly at inlets and outlets of lakes. Wherever relatively (even 2 or 3 degrees above freezing) warm water moves, it erodes and eats away at the ice from underneath. Far too many people seem to have a knack for blundering into such places.

For example, on Moosehead Lake in northern Maine there are several spots that are well-known locally for having no ice or thin ice even in the coldest weather. The two best known and most dangerous are the mouth of Moose River in Rockwood and the area above the East Outlet dam. Yet each winter it can be counted on that they will trap several snowmobilers, and though some may survive the ordeal of cold submersion, some will drown. Some years the incidents are so frequent that the local volunteer fire department (which gets involved in these rescues and body recoveries) has resorted to erecting a rope barrier with signs around the perimeter of the Moose River's mouth.

Even though most of these incidents involve people who are inexperienced or are unfamiliar with the area, those who are familiar with the dangers still get into serious trouble, too. The owner of a cabin in Rockwood, well experienced in ice-fishing on the big lake, stopped his snowmobile one day on the shore prior to heading out for a day's fishing. He briefly chatted with Joe King, a well-known and respected sporting camp owner and guide who for years operated a string of rental ice-fishing shacks on Moosehead. Joe tells the story as follows: It was early January, the first weekend of the new ice-fishing season. The man, who Joe knew well, was pumped up. Season opening is always exciting. The year before, he'd experienced some great fishing on his first outing, and he was eager to repeat the experience.

Deep winter had arrived late to Moosehead country that year. While a shelf of ice formed for a few hundred yards around the edge of the lake, the big area in the center between Moose River and Mount Kineo had remained open until a cold snap skimmed it over with new ice. Joe warned the man of this and urged him not to venture out, but the man knew a hot spot on the Kineo shore, and he was going. (What makes people lose their common sense in search of a few fish?)

Joe, unable to dissuade the man, went back to his work on one of his fish shacks, but he kept an eye on the fisherman as he roared off on a snowmobile, towing his fish traps, ice auger, and other gear on a tote sled. A number of other people fishing along the Rockwood shore also watched him go.

The man, surprisingly, made it out nearly a mile before he ran off the shelf ice and onto the new. Snowmobile, tote sled, and man all disappeared in a splash of water and ice shards. A moment later he bobbed to the surface and began trying to climb back out of the frigid water. Several men tried to get out to him, but in that cold water he soon became unable to struggle. He slipped under before help could get near. Then it became another job for the warden search-and-rescue team.

Because of the thin ice and because the water at that location is more than 200 feet deep, it wasn't possible to do a normal under-ice search, in which dry-suited divers go down with a rope tied securely around their waists so they can find their way back to the hole or be hauled out if they got into trouble. This recovery attempt would differ from previous ones in several respects.

The warden service had begun experimenting with airboats like those used in the Florida Everglades for skimming through shallow water. With no underwater propeller and mounted on a rugged aluminum hull, they could slide over ice, snow, or open water with equal ease. Two airboats were brought into play for this operation. I rode aboard one with the rescue team to film and document the activity for press reporters waiting on shore.

It wasn't difficult finding the spot where the man broke through. Our marker was a floating wooden box that had contained some of his gear. Nearby was an eerie sight: the man's mittens, caught at the edge of the ice where he had attempted to pull himself out. The sight of those empty mittens raised the hair at the back of my neck.

The wardens aboard the two boats used grappling devices made up of large saltwater fishhooks hanging from wooden bars tied to the end of long ropes, which they lowered to the bottom and dragged along as the boats moved in ever-widening circles. They kept this up for several hours, and in time it became evident that this method was not going to work. They anchored a large buoy in place, where it would freeze in and mark the spot. Then we all returned to shore to work on another plan.

Soon, normal winter finally arrived at Moosehead with an arctic blast. The temperature dropped below zero and stayed there, and the ice was deepening on the lake. Now a solid eighteen inches of flinty, blue ice existed where before there had been barely a half-inch. On a brittle-cold, bright winter day the wardens and I set out to the scene again.

This time there would be a substantial departure from the usual search technique. The owner of a marine engineering company in coastal Maine, hearing of the searchers' problems, offered them the use of a self-propelled underwater camera, connected by long waterproof cables to a generator. The controls and television monitor screen were set up in a fish house. One of the wardens cut a hole in the ice with a chain saw, and the device was lowered. We crowded into the little shack to see it in operation. When the camera reached the bottom, the picture quality of the color image appearing on the eight-inch screen was remarkably clear, thanks to the quality of the lens and clarity of Moosehead's water. The monitor even displayed a compass rose, which the experienced operator used, as he said, "to fly" a grid-search pattern.

For some forty-five minutes, as the camera tracked back and forth, we saw only the flat, smooth, silty bottom. But at long last, an object appeared in the distance. As the camera approached we recognized it as an ax with its head stuck down in the silt and the wood handle pointing straight up. Then, as evidence we were following a debris trail, a bait bucket appeared, its lid open. This was soon followed by other items: an ice auger, an ice skimmer, and, suddenly, the snowmobile and sled lying on their sides. Finally, we saw the body itself.

The operator carefully, gingerly steered the camera closer until he could fasten a small pincer on it to the body's snow-mobile suit. Then began the slow ascent as the cable was care-fully pulled back toward the surface. Several guys grouped around the hole, ready to grab the body, but as the body got within a few feet of the surface, the camera pincer lost its grip and the body slowly sank out of sight. The frosty air was rent by frustrated curses. The operator returned to the fish house and resumed his search. Within fifteen minutes he found it again. This time he made sure he had a better grip with the pincer. Again, guys grouped around the hole, some holding grappling hooks. This time, the body came to the surface, was grabbed, and slid onto the ice.

Over the years the dive team made too many of these body recoveries. This elite cadre of dedicated, tough men vol-unteer for this dangerous work, while at the same time serving as full-time district wardens. Rigorous training is required to qualify for the team. During my years at the department, the leader of the team was Warden Sergeant Don Gray. Don is a muscular, rugged guy with a great sense of humor, mischievous grin, and never-failing sense of optimism. He is always gung-ho and ready to cheerfully tackle any tough job, whether in roaring whitewater rapids or under frozen lake ice.

I'm afraid we in the department sometimes took unfair advantage of Don's good nature and willingness to help. The safety officer at the time was Gary Anderson, a man with a fer-tile and creative imagination for disseminating safety messages. Gary would come to me with his ideas and, once or twice a year we'd hatch another scheme that we came to call "Drowning Don Gray."

We had found that television stations were willing to give us lots of free airtime if we supplied them with good, thirty-second public service announcements with a strong safety message. The first of these we set up to not only obtain film footage for a PSA, but we also turned it into a "media event" by inviting newspaper reporters and television news crews. The message was drowning prevention in cold water in the spring-time. We had chosen a spot in the Presumpscot River at the outlet of Sebago Lake. Here there was always open water, even though the lake itself was still ice-covered. Don was to be por-trayed as a fisherman in a small canoe who clumsily tips it over and drowns. Before we started, Don and I stepped aside for a strategy session. I made a suggestion as to how the event could be "spiced up."

As cameras rolled and shutters snapped, Don, a natural actor, played the role to the hilt. As if slightly tipsy he attempted to stand up in the canoe, swayed, and fell over-board, rolling the canoe upside down. Of course, we all knew he was wearing a wet suit under his clothing.

But then, the seconds rolled on, and Don failed to resur-face. The ripples died away, the canoe slowly drifted down-stream, and still no Don. People started looking at each other, raising their eyebrows, asking "Is he all right?" Finally, after what seemed an agonizingly long time, Don popped up and everyone sighed in relief. By now the canoe had drifted a con-siderable distance away in the river's current. Don grasped its rope tender and began towing it back upstream toward us.

Don's "near-drowning" while making the PSA was promi-nently shown on that evening's newscasts, followed by stories in the next day's morning papers. Don and I kept mum about our little deception: When he tipped the canoe over, he rose up under it with his head in the air for breathing. By remaining very still, he was undetectable. Don later confided to me, however, that he had overlooked one important detail: He'd not worn his diving gloves, and within seconds in that frigid water his hands and fingers became so numb he could hardly feel, much less hold, the rope with which he towed the canoe back upstream.

One of the most effective PSAs we produced, which was shown many times daily through the winter months, was on the subject of snowmobile ice safety. Again, it involved fooling the public by "drowning" Don Gray. It showed a snowmobiler (Don, of course) racing erratically around an ice-covered expanse, and crashing and sinking underwater. Many people who saw it on TV were convinced it was an actual drowning that had been caught on videotape.

The crash, filmed at the open outlet of Togus Pond near Augusta, was set up using a second, apparently identical snowmobile that actually was merely a hollow shell. The real snowmobile was set on one side of the open water and the shell on the opposite. A long, thin white rope was tied between the two machines spanning the open water. With Don riding the shell and another warden driving the powered sled, the engine was revved up and Don's sled was snatched forward and pulled into the water, sled and rider dropping swiftly underwater. The shot closed with a close-up shot of bubbles rising to the surface, presumably the rider drowning. This convinced many viewers that they were, indeed, witnessing an actual death. The reality was that Don was again wearing a dive suit under his snowmobiler's coverall and helmet.

One TV spot we produced proved to be too good. It was another Gary/Paul "spectacular." On a small lake near Gray, we had carefully arranged our outdoor "set." We placed a partially submerged canoe in the water. With boat cushions, paddles, etc., floating about, we brought out our "actors." The rescuer was Warden Sergeant Dennis McIntosh—also a member of the SAR dive team. This time he appeared in his warden uniform. The "victim" was Gary Anderson's ten-year-old granddaughter. The scene opened with Dennis scooping the little girl's limp body from the water and rushing ashore past the camera with a stricken look on his face, calling for assistance. Simple, direct, effective. We couldn't have located better actors from Central Casting in Hollywood. Dennis's expression of anguish and turmoil was perfect. The girl's apparently lifeless body was totally convincing—arms dangling loosely, head sagging.

The spot had a very short run on the air. As soon as the stations began running it, they were deluged by callers and complaints: "How can you possibly run pictures of that poor little dead child?" Even when we ran a disclaimer saying it was a staged performance, many people were affected by the realistic images. We tried to convince the stations that the reality of the spot was what made it effective, and that it might save someone's life, but the stations, extremely responsive to viewers' negative reactions, pulled the spot.

While the recovery of drowning victims falls to wardens, so too does searching for lost people, the majority of whom for many years have been hunters. Few experiences can compare with the trauma and despair of getting lost in the woods. Something bad psychologically happens when a person is suddenly cut off from everything they know, and wardens often find that lost hunters get themselves into bizarre predicaments.

Men who otherwise lead normal, reasoned lives suddenly become irrational, even near-insane with panic and fear when they get lost. They've been known to race madly through the woods, throw away their guns and strip off their jackets, sometimes dropping from exhaustion and dying from exposure.

I recall one incident when I was living at Brassua Lake. Warden Norm Harriman was called out to search for a hunter missing near Tarratine. It was well after dark when Norm, using a flashlight, came across the man's tracks in the snow. "He must have been running flat out," Norm told me. "He was making jumps so far apart it was unbelievable." At one point the warden found the man's discarded gun, and later, his coat. When Norm finally reached him, the guy was crawling on hands and knees, hypothermic and whimpering piteously. The man had to be hospitalized in Greenville to recuperate.

Another warden, Eben Perr, racked up a reputation for finding lost hunters. One distraught hunter he was searching for not only got back out to the road, but actually ran right past his own vehicle without noticing it and plunged back into the woods where wardens chased him down.

Guide Tom Arsenault and I once encountered a similar incident. We were guiding a party from upstate New York and hunting in the region of Socatean Stream near Moosehead. These guys had been coming to Maine for years and were experienced hunters. One of their gang, affectionately called "Tubby" because of his girth, never strayed far from camp and mostly stayed on obvious woods roads. No way he'd ever get lost, right? Wrong!

Late one forenoon one of his pals, walking along the road back to camp, heard some thrashing and crashing of brush in a small thicket. Thinking it might be deer flushed by someone else, he prepared to shoot. He was amazed, a moment later, to see Tubby racing pell-mell through the woods, charging wildly through the brush.

He yelled, "Hey, Tubby! What are you doing? What's the matter?"

Tubby never stopped. He yelled: "I gotta go back! I gotta go back!"

It took several of us to catch up to Tubby and stop him. He was in terrible shape: covered in sweat, gasping for breath, and wild-eyed. I feared he was on the verge of a heart attack. We got him back to camp, where he went to bed and spent the rest of the day.

After he'd recovered, he related what happened. A deer had run in front of him. He fired and thought he had hit it, and when it leapt into the woods he plunged in after it. In the heat of the chase, he became completely disoriented. Ironically, the patch of woods he was in was rather small and completely surrounded by woods roads. Had he walked straight in any direction for ten minutes he would have broken out onto a road, but he had lost all rationality. Tubby didn't go hunting again that trip.

Rationality is key when you're lost in the woods. Hunters are told that if they stop as soon as they realize they've lost the way, remain calm, and do a few simple things, they'll soon be found. First, find a bit of shelter from the elements such as a blowdown, ledge, or big tree to cut the wind. If at all possible, build a fire. During the daytime make the fire smoky by piling on leaves, green boughs, etc. Someone will spot it. At night, keep the fire big and bright; haul in firewood before darkness sets in. Not only will it be more visible, both from the ground and air, but it will also keep you warm and provide light to dispel those unseen bugaboos of the night. Best of all, the fire is a living entity; it'll keep you busy and your mind occupied. If you hear gunshots, horns, or sirens and you have ammunition, return the signal (three shots). If you have a whistle, blow it. Both can help guide a warden to you.

One of the most bizarre lost-hunter searches I was involved with began on a snowy day during the last week of the hunting season in late November. An unusually heavy, wind-driven storm cut visibility and piled up drifts. Two feet of snow fell before the storm ended the next day.

It was late in the afternoon of that first day when members of a party staying at a Greenville camp notified the warden headquarters that one of their group had failed to meet at the appointed time and place. They accompanied a couple of wardens to the spot where the man had entered the woods and the search began.

At first, it seemed like it would be another routine search for a hunter who got "turned around" in the blinding snow and whose tracks were covered before he could follow them back out. A big snow day like that would normally end up with several hunters lost throughout the state. Wardens would have most of them out by morning.

But by noon the next day, with no sign or tracks found, it began to look like this was going to be more than routine. I put out the call for volunteers to aid in the search and more wardens were called in. The media became interested. I set up a command post at Greenville Warden Headquarters and began handling media communications.

Then, a great sense of urgency developed. Someone from the lost man's party brought in a couple of the man's medication bottles, and a call to the man's physician in Connecticut disclosed that he was taking medicine for a heart condition. The doctor's opinion was that, given the man's medical problems and the severity of the weather, it was unlikely he could survive for long. A couple other physicians locally concurred: Find him fast or he won't survive.

By now, the media had latched firmly onto the story and were spreading it widely. Volunteer search groups began pouring in from near and far. A group of search-dog handlers from Ohio arrived in a chartered plane and joined the effort. All of this taxed the warden search team to the straining point as it tried to keep the search itself coherent and under control, all while implementing a new search technique.

Using special training received from the National Association for Search and Rescue (NASAR), a search management team considered a number of variables such as the missing person's age and physical condition, terrain features, etc. From there, the team drew up search parameters. Circles were drawn on a map indicating the most likely and lesser likely places where the missing person might be found. Search teams, each headed up by a warden or other experienced person, were then assigned to specific areas to conduct grid searches, in which those searching stretch out in lines so as not to lose sight of the searcher next to them as they look under each brush pile and into each thicket. Others, called "hasty teams," were dispatched to make quick circuits of the search area, looking for tracks or other signs that the victim had managed to get beyond the primary search area. The presumption was that the victim, due to physical limitations, would not get beyond those boundaries. As this case and others would prove, the new search technique was not foolproof.

The hasty teams quickly patrolled the natural boundaries of the search area. First was the road where the hunters had parked their vehicle. While a so-called woods road, this is a major graveled road that runs past Greenville airport and is frequently used by lumbermen, log truck drivers, and locals. Several miles away, forming an unmistakable southern boundary, was a railroad track right-of-way. To the east was a sizable stream that would deter anyone from crossing because they couldn't do it without getting soaked. The west boundary was the airport. The search area was compact, confined, and the man had to be within it.

Some of the force's most experienced and competent wardens were heading up the effort. Parker Tripp was assigned to mapping and radio communications and guys like Pat Dorion, Eric Wight, Steve Hall, Langdon Chandler, Charlie Davis, Mike Collins, and I'm sure others I can't recall, worked long, tough hours, either in search management or leading search teams.

After the fourth day, with not a single track or other sign found, the general consensus was that further ground search was futile. Everyone went home. For the next several days, a warden made a flyover of the area and a district warden surveyed it from a high location. The search had been reduced to "raven patrol," so called because as the vultures of the north, ravens can help wardens locate bodies. Finally, even that effort was abandoned. The hunting season had long since ended. The woods settled down to winter's quiet and solitude. The only hope was that someday the missing man's remains would be found.

Nearly two weeks later, the day winding down on a mid-December afternoon, Chief Warden John March called me with electrifying news. "Are you sitting down?" "Yes I am," I responded, curious. "You're not gonna believe this. That missing hunter is in the Greenville hospital. He just walked out of the woods!" Good thing I was sitting. It was the most incredible thing I'd ever heard.

John told me to get to Greenville immediately. "All hell's gonna bust loose when this gets out!"

Parker Tripp was assigned to drive me to Greenville, but he wasn't told why. He came in my door with a wide grin. "What's up?" I told him. I never saw a man's visage change so instantly from grin to shock; he turned white. It's nearly a two-hour drive from Augusta to Greenville, but that day we made it in a little over one, using the lights and siren when needed to get around traffic. Along the way, we asked each other: "How? How? How?" The man was dead. Or had he somehow faked his death, pulled a giant hoax? There would be many such questions in the coming days, weeks, months—even years. I think some still believe it was a hoax.

When we got to the hospital, I was given permission to go into the resting man's room for just a few minutes to shoot some pictures and videotape to supply the media, who would clamor for some but would not be permitted in the room. I slipped in and began shooting. The hunter was lying quietly, but he gave me a slight smile and seemed alert. In fact, he looked in remarkably good condition for a supposedly sick man who had spent nearly three weeks in the winter woods.

Apparently, a telephone repairman had been driving along the road between the Greenville airport and Wilson Pond when he saw a man, wearing rags wrapped around his feet and a sleeping bag around his shoulders. When the driver stopped by the man and lowered his window, the man politely asked if he could have a ride to Greenville, and when the repairman asked if he was the missing hunter, the man replied that he was.

Shortly after he arrived at the hospital, the hunter told Warden Sergeant Steve Hall and Warden Mike Collins that after he became "turned around," he had wandered for two days through the dense snowfall, with no idea where he was. He said he climbed steep hills (there were none where he had hunted or where the search had been concentrated) and had stumbled into swamps and wet places, filling his rubber boots, which eventually froze around his feet. After several days he came upon the shore of a lake and found an abandoned cabin. He broke a window to get in and soon got a fire going in the stove. He also found some food stashed away.

He stayed in the cabin for several days—he wasn't sure how many—and when the food ran out he decided to try to walk out. Again he wandered aimlessly, ran into more hills, got his feet wet again, and after at least one more night out in the open, he returned to the shore of the lake. He found and entered a second cabin, this one only a few hundred yards along the shore from the first. Again he got a fire going and found more food. He was at this point only a few miles outside Greenville, and, in fact, from the cabin could have seen the rotating beacon at Greenville Airport and the lights of occupied buildings nearby, as well as traffic moving along a road across the pond.

How had the man made his way to the Wilson Pond-Airport road? That morning the lake had been dead calm. Under the camp porch, he had found the hull of a small Sunfish sailboat and dragged it down to the water. Using a board for a paddle, he had made his way down to the end of the pond and found the road where the phone man picked him up.

From the man's description, it wasn't hard for the wardens to deduce that the two cabins were on the east side of Little Wilson Pond, the side with no road, reachable only by water. The next morning, Hall, Collins, and I boarded a seaplane and flew into Wilson Pond to check out the story before meeting with the press. We first landed at the foot of the pond, and sure enough, there was the Sunfish where the man said he'd left it. Then we flew up the lake and landed near some cabins. The first one we came to was obviously the first he'd broken into. The second one was just as the hunter had described, too, and we found further proof that he'd been there: his rifle and his rubber boots, cut open in the back to remove them from his frozen feet. I shot pictures and video of what we found to release to the media.

Later that forenoon I spoke to the hunter, who, surprisingly robust and talkative, pretty much reiterated what he'd told the two wardens the day before. Gangrene had set in to both of his feet, but they didn't need to be amputated. He was, his doctor said, in remarkably good shape. Evidently the reported heart condition had been less serious than previously thought.

Persistent doubts and second-guessing remained. Some still suspected an elaborate hoax had been pulled off. There were rumors that the hunter had been having financial difficulties and meant to fake his death in order to collect on insurance, but lost his nerve. People who knew him, however, said there were no such financial difficulties. There was other speculation, and rumors and plenty of questions. Why hadn't he tried to attract attention? The houses across Wilson Pond were lived in, and their lighted windows were visible from the cabins. Had he walked around the north end of Little Wilson, a distance of only a few miles, he would have come out on an inhabited road. Why not fire his gun? Someone had cut a lot of brush around the last cabin he stayed in; why didn't he set the brush piles on fire to attract attention? Why not set the outhouse on fire, for that matter?

My opinion? I think when the man first became "turned around" on that first snowy day, he lost it mentally. He obviously was not operating rationally. He crossed the big, wide, open road (possibly within yards of his party's vehicle) that was the northern boundary of the search area. Then he wandered around among the hills east of Wilson Pond for several days before stumbling onto the first cabin. There, I suspect he was somewhat out of it, perhaps drifting in and out of an unconscious state induced by the stress. And I have no doubt that it all happened just as he said. The evidence was there to back him up. It was no hoax.

As mysterious as it was, the hunter's case served to reveal a flaw in the NASAR search management concept. It didn't fully account for the variable of individual human actions. I suspect our hunter had crossed that road and become hopelessly confused even before the search effort started. All the effort concentrated in the most likely area had been expended for nothing, as he was never there to be found. The system has since worked admirably in many searches, but it doesn't work every time.

When we think of lost persons, many of us invariably think of hunters. Once, that was true. Wardens told me that until the late eighties and nineties, they would normally expect to be called out two or three nights a week during hunting season.

But then that all changed. One warden in the Greenville area—traditionally one of the busier rescue sites because so many hunters are attracted to the Big Woods there—told me recently that he was called out only a few times during the entire season. And, those hunters who do get lost have become easier to find and are found in better condition than in the past. What happened in the interim? In a word: education.

I like to think it was due in part to the media information the DIFW was cranking out in press releases, magazine stories, and television interviews, but undoubtedly the greatest influence stemmed from the implementation of mandatory hunter safety training courses. All new hunters applying for Maine licenses, as well as those applying who hadn't held a license in the past ten years, are required to attend. The curriculum includes orienteering—the use of map and compass—and woodsmanship—how to take care of yourself in the woods. Quite obviously the training courses are effective, judging by the decrease in the number of lost-hunter cases.

But while the instances of lost hunters has declined, other types of searches are growing in frequency. More people are living in close proximity to wooded areas as the result of urban sprawl, and as a result more people are wandering into the woods and getting lost. This is especially true of those most vulnerable: children and the elderly.

Wardens usually find lost children in short order, but when they don't, the biggest fear is that the child will have to stay out overnight. Younger children, in particular, don't know how to take care of themselves in those cases. But luckily, some children do.

I remember one search for a young brother and sister who disappeared from the yard of their home in North Livermore.

Wardens and volunteers searched the dense woods in the area for the remainder of the day and through the night. Fearing the worst might have befallen the children, the search was greatly intensified at daylight, when more volunteers answered the call and showed up in force.

A search team located the siblings by mid-morning. They were sitting on a rock where they had spent the night, cuddling to keep warm and entertaining each other with rhymes and fairy tales. Seems these kids handled their situation better than many adults do.

At the other end of the spectrum are the seniors. A large number of the elderly, most of them suffering from dementia or Alzheimer's, wander into the woods, which shouldn't be too surprising in a state that is 90 percent forested. The problem with these victims is that their behavior can be very unpredictable. One of the most pitiable incidents I remember involved an elderly lady we'll call Dolly.

Dolly drove away from her home in Lincoln and disappeared. State police started a missing person search. After the media picked up the story, a strange report came in. A man said that on the day Dolly vanished, he and a friend were chatting in front of a country store near the intersection of Routes 1 and 6 in eastern Washington County. An older woman drove up in a yellow car matching the description of Dolly's. She asked: "Excuse me, could you please tell me how to get to Lincoln?" "Sure. Just go to the corner there and turn left," one of the men answered.

The woman thanked them and drove off. The men saw her stop at the intersection. Shortly after, she turned around and came back. As though she'd never been there, she asked: "Excuse me, could you tell me how to get to Lincoln?" The man said, "Lady, I just told you. Go to the corner and turn left, and that road will bring you right to Lincoln!"

Again she thanked him politely and drove off. The men watched as this time she stopped at the intersection and then turned right, in the opposite direction of Lincoln.

The search immediately shifted to that twenty-mile section of Route 6 from Route 1 to Vanceboro at the Maine–New Brunswick boundary, where border guards determined that Dolly had not crossed into Canada.

It didn't take long for someone to spot Dolly's vehicle. It was a couple of miles up a side road, parked and abandoned. There was no sign of her. How did she end up there? That particular secondary road, used mainly by lumbermen, branches off at a curve in the main roadway. It was later theorized that, seeing the road continue straight ahead, Dolly in her confused state chose to continue on it rather than follow the curve, even though the side road was obviously in inferior condition.

This new development immediately put the search into the jurisdiction of the warden service. Wardens and volunteers converged from all over the state. A command post was set up near the tiny community of Lambert Lake, and in short order, grid searches and hasty teams were deployed, beginning where the vehicle had been found and radiating out. Surely this small, elderly lady could not travel too far, could she?

For two days and nights the searchers scoured the surrounding forest and found nary a sign of Dolly. Then some disturbing reports began filtering in. Ten miles from the scene, someone found a newspaper clipping of an obituary. Dolly's family had reported that she frequently clipped obits—even of people she never knew—and carried them around in her purse. How did that clipping get there? And could this feeble little lady have traveled so far? A portion of the search was moved to that area, but nothing else was found.

Then other curious reports came into the command post. Several people driving in the area along Route 6 at various times said they had seen a woman at the roadside. When they got near her she turned and ran into the woods. It had to be Dolly.

It wasn't until late in the afternoon of the third day that a grid-search team found a footprint in a soft spot on the ground: a small, bare footprint. A few other prints were found a short distance away. Soon they came upon Dolly's jacket, hung up on the stub of a tree branch. By then, the radios were crackling; they must be getting close. They weren't too far from Route 6, and an ambulance was dispatched to stand ready.

Finally, the searchers reached Dolly. She was sitting on a rock, hunched down, head in her hands, and whimpering and sobbing incoherently. Searchers made out the words: "Where's my mommy?" They whisked Dolly away to be checked out at the nearest hospital.

The search for Dolly was long, but fortunately it was a success.

Of course, today's global positioning systems and personal locator beacons, as one official says, are taking the search out of search and rescue. In some places, residents can borrow a PLB from the local fire station before making their trip into the woods or other remote area. With the price of technology falling, it won't be long before such devices are compact and cheap enough for everyone. If there's one thing I learned, though, during my years at the Fish and Wildlife department, it's that the dedication and experience of Maine's hardworking wardens can never be replaced.

Flying Wardens

In over a half-century of flying—as either pilot or passenger—the closest I ever came to losing my breakfast was on a bitter-cold, blustery January day over the rugged coast of Maine.

I was in the rear seat of a Cessna Skymaster, selected for its twin fore-and-aft engines to provide redundant safety in the event we lost one. Handling the controls in the left front seat was George Later, then chief pilot for the Maine Warden Service. Riding shotgun was Skip Spencer, wildlife biologist for the Maine Department of Inland Fisheries and Wildlife. We were flying at low altitude along the craggy, spray-battered coast of Mount Desert Island and Acadia National Park. Later and Spencer were counting ducks as part of the annual mid-winter census of waterfowl wintering along Maine's coast. Why these ducks, geese, and sea ducks choose to winter in these frigid waters among ice floes is something known only to the birds.

While Later wheeled and turned and ducked into and out of coves and bays past steep rocky cliffs, Spencer intently gazed down over the side of the craft and calmly intoned species and numbers into the microphone of a tape recorder on his lap. Spencer and his assistants would later transcribe these recorded notes into data forms and use them for comparison with previous years' counts for compiling population trends. As for myself, I was along to film this activity. Flying and filming were something I engaged in rather frequently, so what made this flight so different from the norm? I recall three reasons. In the bitter cold, the plane's windows, especially in the rear where I was trying to film, kept icing up and obscuring the view. George cranked the heat up to max in an attempt to clear them. The result? While it was below zero outside, inside the Cessna it was stifling. Second, both of these guys were chain-smokers, and the cockpit—this was back in the days that this was allowed—was filled with smoke. Finally, the near-severe turbulence as we bounced around, the steep turns and banks, and the fact I was looking through the viewfinder of a movie camera combined for the most ideal conditions for vertigo I've ever experienced. That was one time when I was very grateful to climb out of a plane and feel solid ground and breathe in great gulps of that good, cold Maine winter air.

That bird-counting mission was just another day at the office, though, for warden pilot George Later. The Maine Warden Service, a division of Inland Fisheries and Wildlife, has by necessity used aircraft in its activities for many decades. The state is large and up to 90 percent of its 33,000 square miles are forested, much of it isolated. With a relatively small warden service comprised of about a hundred thinly spread wardens, using aircraft is a must.

Today, the state's three warden pilots in their Cessna 185s are kept busy. In early May and October, they stock a quarter of a million fish in some 150 of Maine's isolated and remote lakes and ponds that are otherwise inaccessible. Up to three hundred to 350 fish of legal size—mostly brook trout, but also some landlocked salmon and splake (a brook/lake trout hybrid)—can be carried in specially designed tanks bolted to each of the plane's pontoons. Once over the stocking site, flying at about eighty knots and at a treetop height of about seventy to eighty feet, the pilot flips a switch and empties one or both of the tanks. The fish hit the water with a splash and instantly disappear. Research has shown that most survive the drop.

During the rest of the year, the majority of the warden pilots' work focuses on search and rescue and protecting the state's fish and wildlife resources.

As noted in the previous chapter about my experiences at the Department of Inland Fisheries and Wildlife, people who find their way into Maine's seventeen million acres of forests seem to have a propensity for getting lost. Be they a youngster who wandered away from preoccupied parents, a hunter or hiker who strayed off the trail, or a confused Alzheimer's patient, if wardens can't locate them after a few hours of ground search, warden pilots are called in to assist. They not only fly searchers and equipment to remote sites when needed, but they usually also fly over the search area themselves. Often it's the warden pilot who first spots the lost person, especially if that person has the presence of mind to build a fire or move to a clearing where he/she can be more easily spotted.

Their job is not always that easy. Warden pilots are called on to locate sick or injured campers in remote areas. They fly in to inform healthy campers in a remote area that there's a serious illness or death at home. Sometimes the warden pilot's job is to retrieve the bodies of drowning or accident victims, and sometimes the job is gruesome. Pilot Andy Stinson once had to fly out the body of a man frozen in such a grotesque position that it couldn't fit in a body bag or inside the cockpit and had to be tied to the top of the pontoon.

Warden pilots also can arrive just in the nick of time to save lives. Dana Toothaker was once flying past a lake on another mission when he heard a radio call that a person on that very lake had fallen from a capsized boat and was in danger of drowning. Scanning the lake surface, Dana spotted the victim. Within seconds, he had glided down to a landing alongside the surprised victim, helped him onto his pontoon, and taxied him safely to shore to the amazement of would-be rescuers.

In addition to piloting skills, Dana was blessed with super-sharp eyesight. From the air, he once located the body of a drowning victim that had washed under a pile of driftwood along a shore. Only a bit of the man's leg was visible. One dark night he was called out to search for a lost hunter. The hunter, in trying to cross a boggy area, had stepped into a deep hole and plunged into ice-cold water up to his chest. He couldn't feel any higher footing from his position and he didn't dare move lest he step into even deeper water. He was stuck. When he eventually heard a plane approaching overhead, he snapped on his cigarette lighter—the only signaling device he had— and held it above his head. That feeble flame was enough to catch Dana's keen eye. He directed ground wardens to the hunter's rescue.

Veteran game warden pilot Jack McPhee was known for his keen eye, too. He patrolled the big woods of northern Maine for two decades and earned a legendary reputation. Based at Eagle Lake, his "beat" was the Allagash Wilderness, where he chalked up some impressive recoveries. One I recall was a teenage boy hunting alone who failed to come out of the woods at dark. It was late in deer-hunting season, bitterly cold and with a foot of snow covering the ground. Jack flew for a couple hours over the dark forest before he spotted a tiny glimpse of light below. The boy had managed to gather a few dry twigs and set them afire. The flame only lasted a few seconds, but that was long enough for Jack to spot it. He radioed the boy's location to wardens on the ground. It was such a cold night, the boy's rescuers doubted he could have survived until morning.

Late one afternoon, Jack was called out to look for an out-of-state hunter who got lost during a wet, sticky snowstorm. Flying conditions were so bad that he was almost forced to give up, but he persisted. The hunter, meanwhile, had wandered into an abandoned lumber camp yard. When he heard the plane circling close by, he searched desperately for something dry with which to start a fire. He found a few relatively dry boards in a collapsed building, but no tinder for a fire-starter. In desperation he pulled out his wallet and removed the only dry thing he could find: paper money. Igniting it with his lighter, he managed to get a small, smoky fire going. Jack spotted it, and directed a ground warden to the site. The rescued man later admitted he had burned up some $300. "But it was well worth it!"

Of course, wardens are primarily law enforcement officers. Warden pilots land on bodies of water—whether on skis in the winter or floats in the summer—to check for proper licenses, bag limits, and violations of boating safety regulations, such as not having proper personal flotation devices on board. They also spend many hours aloft serving as spotters for the local district wardens. From the air, they can keep ground wardens informed of unusual concentrations of hunters' vehicles along remote roads and report any other suspicious activity. Wardens also go on surveillance for illegal night deer hunters—poachers or "jackers," who often use powerful spotlights to "freeze" normally skittish deer.

When a spate of night-hunting was reported along a country road in a sparsely populated section of central Maine, I went on a stakeout with two wardens. We took up our positions at the back of a field; other teams were set up at promising locations within a few miles of us. Eagle-eyed Dana Toothaker was several thousand feet above us on the lookout for any unusual lighting activity. Radio silence was observed as much as possible; if communication was necessary, codes and map grids were used as minimally as possible. Savvy poachers have been known to use radio monitors to try to keep track of wardens' whereabouts. My two companions were veterans of many such exercises and had many close calls with poachers, some of whom were fueled by alcohol. Poachers had chased them through the woods and tried to run them down with their vehicles.

During this stakeout, we received a coded warning from the plane: A suspicious vehicle was headed our way. Soon, sure enough, headlights appeared, and a pickup moved slowly up the road. It came to a stop and a powerful searchlight began scanning the field. From our vantage point we couldn't see if there were deer in the field, but there apparently was at least one because the night's silence was suddenly shattered by a tremendous blast from a high-powered firearm. The spotlight shone for several more minutes, until someone in the truck, evidently deciding he'd missed, doused it and continued driving up the road.

The wardens and I headed for our vehicle and, without putting on the headlights, took off bouncing across the field. Toothaker kept us apprised of the truck's progress. When we reached the road we kept our lights off and sped toward the truck with its still-unsuspecting occupants. As we came up behind it, we snapped on the headlights, the flashing blues, and the siren. Then we whipped around in front of the pickup and skidded to a stop, barring its way.

Within minutes, other wardens who had been stationed nearby showed up and surrounded the truck and its surprised occupants. A search of the truck turned up firearms, spent shell casings, live ammo, opened beer containers, and parts of illegal game. The suspects were read their rights and taken in hand-cuffs to the nearest police station to face charges. Meanwhile, the wardens, including Dana Toothaker in his plane, returned to their vigils for the rest of the night.

Deer are also at risk from dogs. In late winter when snow is the deepest and deer, by now often hungry and weak, are most vulnerable, wardens spend many days on snowshoes, on snow-mobiles, and in the air, trying to find and capture the dogs that chase and terrorize them. When chased, the deer are forced to leave their trodden paths and plunge into the deep snow. Well-fed dogs—family pets—are strong and fast and can skim over snow where the plunging deers' sharp hooves break through. The overstressed, floundering deer are soon exhausted and become easy victims. Such scenes can be horrifying, with blood-smeared snow and deer body parts scattered about. Dogs usually attack from the rear and chew the deer's haunches to the point where the deer is unable to move, leaving them to suffer an agonizing, lingering death. Even if a chased deer is not caught, it can be stressed to the point where it develops a form of pneumonia and then dies.

Flying wardens spot the dogs and direct ground troops to their location. Wardens have the authority to destroy dogs caught in the act of harassing deer, but prefer to capture them and return them to their owners, who are fined and warned to keep their dogs under control.

I was with Toothaker on such a mission when we saw a huge, dark dog (possibly a rottweiler) emerging from the woods. As we swooped down low over it, the big brute began leaping and snapping its jaws at us. I shudder to think what it would have done to us if we were on the ground.

Despite so many thousands of hours of flying in often stressful and hazardous conditions over remote, wild terrain, the warden flying service has compiled an impressive safety record, with only a few fatalities, two of them in the distant past.

On August 27, 1956, pilot George F. Townsend took off from Maranacook Lake in Winthrop in his just recently acquired Cessna 180. Witnesses said they saw the plane nose up steeply just after takeoff. It stalled and crashed into the lake, killing George and his passenger, a department biologist. The prevailing theory for the crash: The pilot's seat came unlatched and slid back and George instinctively clung to the yoke, with no time for recovery.

On September 27, 1972, astonishingly at the same lake, pilot Richard E. Varney, piloting a Bell helicopter, was landing at a dock to refuel when he apparently lost power and dropped into the lake. A nonswimmer, he drowned only a short distance from shore. Prevailing theory: It was a chilly, damp morning and the carburetor iced up, causing loss of power.

Jack McPhee, who was long since retired and no longer officially a warden pilot at the time, lost his life on May 5, 2003, when his plane crashed near Third Musquacook Lake while he was monitoring radio-collared lynxes. Prevailing theory: A medical crisis, rather than pilot error or plane malfunction, caused the crash.

Daryl Gordon, a twenty-five-year warden and department pilot since 2004, died on March 25, 2011, when his plane crashed on the ice of Clear Lake in the Allagash Region. That accident was under investigation at the time of this writing.

The current three-man Maine Warden Service flying corps, now headed by the latest Later, Charlie, has some mighty big shoes to fill. Not least of those are the shoes of Charlie's late dad, George, who left a huge legacy in the history of the Maine Warden Service pilot force. Considering the vital roles they play and the services they provide, it appears that Maine will be relying on the skills of its flying wardens well into the future.

Foster Eagle

The three-month-old eaglet fidgeted with suppressed
energy on its pine limb perch sixty feet above Swan
Island in Maine's Kennebec River. The young bird
was an impressive sight. It had reached its full growth and
appeared to loom even larger than its parents, but it lacked
their darker body plumage and the strikingly regal white-feath-
ered head and tail of the adult American bald eagle. It stood
over three feet tall on big, powerful, long-clawed yellow feet,
and its wingspan exceeded seven feet. Even at this young age it
had the wickedly curved raptorial beak of the eagles that have
for centuries have adorned the scepters of kings, the standards
of great armies, and the seals of great nations.

The young eagle walked awkwardly out to the end of the
big limb, wings flopping incongruously as the branch bent and
trembled under its weight, much like a cartoon caricature of a
clown tightrope walker struggling to maintain balance. Then, it
launched itself into a shallow dive, tail flared widely and big
wings beating rhythmically to attain flying speed.

It sailed out over a freshly planted field of rye, where sunlight reflected from the fresh earth created a rising column of
warm air called a thermal. Higher, two adult eagles were soar-
ing in wide, lazy circles, their dark bodies and white heads and

tails etched starkly against the blue sky. The young eagle rode up the thermal to join them.

Watching through the viewfinder of a telephoto-lensed movie camera, I could see the brownish-gray feathers rippling on the young eagle's breast as it slowly, gracefully, spiraled upward. The long, strong primary feathers at its wingtips— over which the eagle has individual control—were bent upward and splayed out to feel and capture every nuance of lift from the rising air. The young eagle had made its first flight less than two weeks before, but already it was mastering flight techniques with sure, instinctive confidence.

There was no great crowd to view and cheer this epic event, but there should have been. This was no ordinary eaglet. To a small handful of dedicated wildlife researchers, it was the symbol of success and hope for the future.

These eagle parents could not have brought forth this young eagle on their own because within their bodies were heavy concentrations of deadly poisons—the residues of persistent pesticides with which humans had been saturating the planet for decades. The poison had become concentrated in the fish the eagles ate, and was accumulating in their brains and body fats. It had rendered them sterile; the eggs they laid each spring in their high aerie would rot and never hatch. Eventually, the toxins would kill the adult eagles as well.

The life of this young eagle had been sparked early that spring, 1,500 miles away, when its natural parents mated in the branches of a tall tree in the Chippewa National Forest in the snowy north woods of northern Minnesota. The resulting egg was removed from their nest in a tall aspen tree and gently and swiftly transplanted to Maine where it was placed in the aging eagle pair's nest. The old pair had previously been brooding a lone egg for weeks; that unproductive egg was later found to contain one of the highest concentrations of pesticide residues ever found in an egg. It was only by means of the transplant that these eagles could become parents.

By the early 1970s, Maine's bald eagle population, once numbering in the thousands, had dwindled and was on the verge of total extirpation. Populations in the rest of the United States were dire as well. The Minnesota-to-Maine egg-transplant operation—the first time such a transplant was ever attempted—and others like it helped to save the bald eagle from extinction.

Biologist Frank Gramlich and others in the U.S. Fish and Wildlife Service had been talking about attempting such a transplant as a solution to Maine's eagle problem for several years. The elements finally fell into place in the spring of 1974. By late winter, Gramlich had selected several active candidate nests in the production area around the lower Kennebec River. The team had hoped to make the egg transplant early in the breeding season, but bad weather and other obstacles had prevented that from happening. By the time the transplant was attempted in early May, seven pairs of eagles had already abandoned their nests, likely discouraged by the lack of life within their eggs (if they had laid eggs at all), or with the thin-shelled eggs already broken in the nest.

On May 3, U.S. Fish and Wildlife biologist Paul Nickerson met up with a young graduate student, Dave Evans, at Chippewa National Forest, where no pesticide spraying had ever occurred. With Nickerson supervising, Evans, an accomplished tree climber and eagle-bander, climbed several selected nest trees and removed smooth, creamy-white, obviously healthy eggs. He carefully packed the eggs into a tissue-lined container and lowered them by rope to Nickerson. Above Nickerson's head, the adult eagles wheeled and screeched in protest. It was believed they would later lay a fresh clutch of eggs into their empty nest.

Nickerson had hoped to gather at least a half-dozen eggs, but climbing conditions were not the best that day. Most of the selected nests were in tall aspen trees, and a light-falling rain made the smooth bark slippery. Evans had safely retrieved three eggs and was going for more when he slipped from a tree and fell to the ground, narrowly escaping serious injury. Nickerson called a halt to the climbing. He'd have to go with just three good eggs.

The eggs were gently placed into a small suitcase that had been converted into a portable incubator heated by a rubber hot bottle. A thermometer was stuck up through a hole in the lid for monitoring the inside temperature. When it got too hot for the eggs, the temperature was regulated simply by opening the lid to allow heat to escape.

That night, gingerly carrying their incubator as though it were a touchy live bomb, Nickerson and Evans boarded a flight out of Minnesota to Boston. Since there were no connecting night flights from Boston to Maine, they rented a car at Logan International Airport and drove the 150 miles in the middle of the night to Maine's capital, Augusta. Gramlich was waiting for the men when they arrived. While they snatched a few hours' sleep, he took over the duty of monitoring the incubator temperature.

Early the next morning I met the three men at the Augusta headquarters of the Maine Department of Inland Fisheries and Wildlife, which was cooperating with the Fish and Wildlife

Service in the transplant program. I was under contract to go along and film the transplant operation.

Accompanied by a couple of guys from the Fish and Wildlife Department and professional tree climber Bob Barr, the group departed for the first nesting site some ten miles south of Augusta on Nehumpkeag Island. Nehumpkeag is a small, wooded mound barely an acre in size situated in the middle of the Kennebec at South Gardiner. The nest was located near the very tip of the tallest tree on the island, a stately pine. As we made our way through thick brush to reach the base of the big pine tree, we saw the adult eagle retreat to the shore and perch on a dying elm tree to watch this invasion of her home.

The transplant crew lost little time, keeping the interruption as brief as possible. Using climbing spurs and a rope, Barr swiftly and expertly ascended the tree and climbed into the nest—not an easy chore, as the huge nest formed an umbrella-like canopy at the top of the tree, and he had to climb out and up around its edge. Inside he found a small, brown egg. "It feels awfully light, like a Ping-Pong ball. It feels empty," he shouted down to us.

On the ground, Nickerson and Gramlich were carefully preparing the first viable white Minnesota egg for its journey up the tree. They placed the egg in a tissue-lined cardboard box, which was then placed into a knapsack. The pack was tied with great care to a rope Barr had lowered to the ground. On a signal from Nickerson, Barr slowly, carefully began pulling the rope with its fragile cargo up through the branches so that it wouldn't jar on the way up. Within a few minutes he had safely pulled the backpack up into the nest, opened it, removed the egg, and placed it gently in the nest at the spot occupied by the original egg. That egg he then placed into the box and sack, and lowered it slowly down to Gramlich and Nickerson.

"Let's not hang around here any longer than we have to," Nickerson said. "I don't want the adult to be scared away so that the egg chills too much or she abandons the nest."

We could still see the adult sitting on the dead elm watching our shenanigans. We lost no time in leaving. The overriding worry in our minds: Had all this commotion been too much for the eagle, and would she fear returning to her nest? And how would she react to the new white egg replacing her brown one? These questions would have to remain unanswered for the next several hours, as we drove toward our next transplant tree.

Swan Island, about five miles long and one mile wide, lies in the Kennebec River about twenty miles south of Augusta, at the head of Merrymeeting Bay. This is tidewater; the estuarine environment created by the shallow bay—with its vast acreages of wild rice, marshes, and five rivers which empty into it—makes it a unique place for wildlife. Thousands of wild geese and ducks rest and feed in the bay during spring and fall migrations. Several waterfowl species nest in the region.

The island has long been home to eagles, and, in fact, historical scholars believe the name "Swan" (earlier called "Swango") is a white man's corruption of the Abenaki Indian name for the bald eagle *Sowangan*. Since 1940, the island has been a wildlife preserve managed by the Fish and Wildlife department. At the time of the egg transplant, there was one remaining bald eagle nest on the island.

We were met at the boat landing in Richmond by the island's head guardian, Bob Whitman, and we rode across the channel in his big scow, normally used for hauling supplies and equipment. Upon landing, Whitman took us by stake-body truck about three miles. The nest, located about midway down the island, was in a giant, gnarled oak tree on a high knoll, one of the highest spots on the island.

Our arrival was greeted by the usual cries of alarm as the adult eagles flew from the nest and began circling over our heads. Our crew, with the experience of one successful transplant, approached the nest with purpose and dispatch. Within minutes, Barr was up the tree and into the nest.

"There's one egg," he informed us. He picked it up and added: "This one's empty, too. But it's got something hard rattling inside of it," he added, holding the egg up to his ear.

Barr then started to haul up the second white Minnesota egg. The transplant was going well. Perhaps too smoothly? He made the transfer of eggs in the nest and lowered the bad egg to the ground without a hitch. He began to climb out of the nest.

Old eagles' nests are huge conglomerations of big and small sticks, leaves, debris, and grasses all woven together. Many, including the Swan Island nest, are used for years, with new additions made each spring. Some grow to weigh hundreds of pounds, or even tons. Sometimes they lead to the early death of the tree in which they're built.

The Swan Island nest was huge. Unlike many Maine eagle nests that are built near the topmost branches of large pine trees (usually the tallest tree), this one was situated about two-thirds of the way up the big oak, where the main trunk split into several heavy branches forming a convenient building platform. Limbs and branches formed a canopy over it.

A foster parent returns to the aerie on Swan Island.

I watched Barr struggling to climb over the edge of the nest, but then he stopped. I heard him mutter: "Uh-oh! You guys ain't gonna believe this!"

Nickerson, sensing trouble, stood up from where he was packing the incubator and asked: "What happened?"

"A dead limb just fell from above into the nest and hit the egg."

"Did it break?" asked Nickerson.

"Yeah. It's got a crack!"

Nickerson and Gramlich held a brief council. They had one good Minnesota egg remaining, which they had intended to place in a third eagle nest on Merrymeeting Bay. But that nest had been their third choice because its eagle pair had been behaving erratically and not brooding well, and they feared the eagles were on the verge of abandoning it. They decided to put the last egg in the nest at hand. It was well-protected and easy to observe, and the eagles it belonged to were a good nesting pair.

And so in short order the last viable Minnesota egg was hauled up and placed in the nest's "cup." The damaged egg was removed and settled into the cradling incubator.

We were concerned and anxious as we departed Swan Island. We were all too aware that if the adult eagles were too long in returning to brood the transplanted eggs, they might chill and die. Gramlich had arranged for his assistant, Linda Wright, a graduate student in wildlife resources at the University of Maine, to observe the Swan Island nest with a powerful scope from a distance. A neighbor had agreed to watch the Nehumpkeag birds to see if they would return to the nest.

Later, the reports from the two observers were good: The birds had returned and resumed brooding the eggs within thirty-five minutes of our departure from both sites. We then began the long period of waiting to see if the birds would stick to the brooding and successfully hatch out the eggs.

In mid-May both transplanted eggs had hatched. It's believed it was the first time in history that this had been successfully accomplished by bald eagles.

When the youngsters were two weeks old, I began spending a bit of time watching and photographing the Nehumpkeag nest, usually filming toward sunset when the eagles were feeding and active before settling in for the night. Once I saw and photographed the male being chased up the river toward the nest by an osprey. This was a real switch, since eagles traditionally have used ospreys as their fish catchers. Ospreys (aka, fish hawks) are much better at diving into the water and catching live fish than are bald eagles. The eagles, being larger and stronger, wait until the osprey is heading back toward its own nest with a heavy fish and then attack it, forcing the osprey to drop the fish. (This also works against seagulls.) The eagle then swoops down and snatches the falling fish.

When the male returned to his aerie, he spent several minutes feeding his mate, tearing off chunks of fish he had caught and offering them to her in his beak. Then both adults fed the youngster, lowering their heads far down into the nest, with fanned-out white tails pointing up, as they stuffed bits of fish into the eaglet's mouth.

Finally the female eased herself down upon her youngster with the movements familiar to anyone who has ever observed a hen settling down to brood her chicks. Pop perched at the edge of the nest, looking out over the open river where he could observe any approaching danger. There they stayed as nightfall descended over the Kennebec Valley.

Severe weather hit Maine during the last week of May. Heavy rains slashed the state, sending streams and rivers over their banks and flooding lowlands. Winds of near-gale force roared off the Atlantic Ocean and buffeted the state for days. Low clouds obscured visibility. Those of us who were "eagle watching" waited out this period with impatience and frustration. When the stormy weather began abating about a week later, we received a depressing report from Linda Wright: The Nehumpkeag eagles had abandoned their nest.

Bob Barr climbed again and found the nest empty. No trace of the eaglet was found. Whatever had befallen it, we'd never know. Gramlich didn't rule out the possibility that the young bird may have become wet and chilled during the stormy weather and died of exposure. It might have been blown out of the nest by the strong winds. Or, a large bird of prey, such as a hawk, owl, or osprey, might have chanced upon the eaglet during an unprotected moment and snatched it.

Our attentions turned to the remaining eaglet in its Swan Island nest. In early June, I took my camera gear and a small, portable blind to the island. I set up the blind in an inconspicuous spot under some trees a couple of hundred feet from the nest. These eagles were used to work crews driving past on the island road, so I hoped they'd accept me as a routine part of island life. From the rear of the blind, I could see a small herd of deer feeding in a rye field, paying no attention to the eagles or the blind.

I hoped to photograph the lone surviving transplant eaglet with both movies and still photos. The baby was still susceptible to so many possible tragedies, and we wanted to obtain photographic proof of the successful hatching.

At first, the adults didn't seem overly distraught about my blind. The male perched on his favorite large dead limb on a tall white pine tree a hundred feet from the nest. The female perched in the oak above the nest. Now and then she flew off and circled overhead, uttering soft, squeaky calls: *squee, squee.* Eagle calls have been likened to a board nail being pulled out. To me, they resemble the sound of my neighbor's fence when one of his cows pokes her head through and strains the fence to reach the vegetables in our garden.

Inside the blind I focused my cameras on the nest. The eaglet must have been dozing; nothing happened for an hour or more. Then (naturally), when I was relaxed and off guard, a small, dark shape bobbed up, and a tiny wing flipped up and out of sight again. I missed the shot. Within a few minutes the eaglet moved again. I never did get a good look at the bird, which kept itself behind a large limb, but after several more bobbings I felt I'd captured it on film—if only fleetingly.

I kept on peering intently through the viewfinder, with my finger ready to fire off a burst of film at any movement, when a sharp snort and foot stamp just behind the blind startled me. I swiveled around to find a young buck deer, antlers half-grown and covered in velvet, about twenty feet from the blind. The buck snorted again (an explosive expelling of air aimed at alerting other deer), threw up its white tail, and danced off perhaps thirty feet.

Deer are curious. The buck lowered his head and cautiously approached the blind a second time. By now, the other deer in the field were watching, heads up and alert. The buck snorted explosively and bolted, his white tail highly erect and startlingly white, a sure sign of alarm to all creatures. The herd in the field streaked away in a blur of graceful leaps and white tails. The eagles took wing and began circling, calling anxiously.

My presence had been betrayed.

By now the adult eagles were thoroughly alarmed. They circled and wheeled overhead, uttering the shrill squeaking cry and also a lower *kuk, kuk* call. The female would alight in the top of the nest tree, throw her head back and call loudly, and then take wing again. The eaglet remained out of sight down in the nest.

I packed everything up and left immediately so as not to create more of a disturbance.

Reviewing the film later I found that I had captured a brief movie shot of the eaglet's wing fluttering but no good still photograph to prove the eaglet's existence.

Bill Snow was at the time the Maine state conservation agent for the U.S. Fish and Wildlife Service and pilot for its Northeastern U.S. Region. He was preparing to make an over-flight of Maine eagle nests to count the young of the year, and he offered to take me up to see if we could get a picture of the Swan Island eaglet from the air. As an ex–bush pilot, how could I refuse?

Snow followed the Kennebec River down from his home base at the Waterville Airport, and as we passed South Gardiner we swooped low so I could grab shots of the Nehumpkeag Island nest. High and open to view, the nest was indeed empty, and there were no signs of the adults in the area.

We had been delayed in making this flight at least a week due to poor flying weather. Once over Swan Island, we found the delay was to our detriment. The leaves of the big nest oak were now almost full-grown, forming an obscuring canopy of green above the nest. Flying over it at low altitude, we could see the adult sitting on the edge of the nest, but we weren't certain if we could see the dark youngster or not. Even at the relatively slow flying speed of eighty miles per hour required to keep the heavy plane airborne and under safe control, the nest flashed by with fleeting swiftness, allowing only a brief glance.

It was tough to tell just what I was getting for pictures. As it turned out, most of the still slides I shot were fairly good pictures of a tree, but you couldn't see into the nest for the leaves. We lucked out with one shot I made just as a hole opened up. The adult is plainly seen sitting on one side of the nest. Opposite her is the smaller lump: her foster child.

In mid-June, several of us from the original transplanting crew gathered on Swan Island. Our mission: to remove the

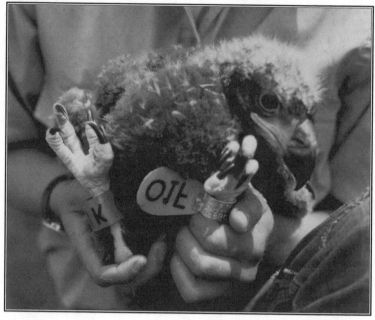

Paul Fournier/Courtesy Maine State Museum

The month-old eaglet was successfully banded while its foster parents circled nervously overhead.

month-old eaglet from the nest, examine and band it, and return it safely to its nest.

The eaglet displayed no fright or concern as it was placed in a knapsack and lowered to the ground, and appeared completely calm after it landed. It was a ludicrously comic-looking creature that appeared from within that bag, all beak and big eyes and huge yellow feet. Kinky-tight gray down covered its round, fat butterball body. Obviously its foster parents—now circling nervously overhead—had been feeding it well. Further evidence of that was provided by Bob Barr, who shouted down to us that there were two large, uneaten eels in the nest.

Once the banding was completed and we had taken our pictures, the eaglet was on its way back up to the aerie in the canvas bag.

A month later, the eaglet began to feather out and take on the regal look of its ancestry. Its foster parents were not spending as much time at the nest now. Most of their day was spent roosting in trees along the shore, where they could keep an eye on the nest and youngster and also watch for floating food. They paid no mind to workers on the island who were plowing and reseeding nearby rye fields, or to the tractors and trucks roaring back and forth all day. By now they apparently recognized me as harmless as well. I no longer required the blind and would simply set up at the base of some trees where I could blend in with the background, ready should any action unfold.

Most of the time there simply wasn't any action to record. The parents fed the youngster early in the morning, before there was sufficient light for photography. The remainder of the day they drowsed in their roost trees. ("Eagles are great loiterers," a biologist once told me.) The youngster, meanwhile, kept itself out of sight down in the nest, or sat for hours looking vacantly out across the field.

As July progressed, I observed subtle changes in the eaglet's appearance and behavior. It was fully feathered out now, an overall dark brown with lighter blotches, particularly on the breast. Despite its large size (now about equal to its parents), the bird was difficult to spot when sitting on the edge of the nest or against the tree trunk. The splotchy plumage made good camouflage, and the bird blended in among the leaves and sun-spotted branches. The eagle's beak had developed the curved hook characteristic of raptors. And its big, piercing eyes were becoming alert and more aware of objects away from the immediate nest area.

At about this time I recorded on film a true milestone in the life and development of this young eagle. The youngster began to fidget and move about the nest. It extended and retracted its wings—now amazingly long and beautifully shaped. It walked about the nest, stretching and peering about and opening its mouth wide, but uttering no sound that I could hear. I followed its every move, eye glued to viewfinder and film rolling. The bird sidled up to the edge of the nest nearest where I was positioned. With a 400mm lens on the camera, the bird was enlarged so that it appeared only a few feet away from me. I critically adjusted the focus and kept the movie camera rolling, lest I miss some significant action. The eaglet turned to face away from me, and began slowly lowering its head. I was tense at the camera, finger pressing the release button. The bird's head dipped down out of sight as its tail rose higher and higher. I was looking right up under the fanned tail feathers. Then the eagle voided its bowel, squirting out an explosive stream of chalky excrement. I flinched instinctively, so close did it appear. The joke—if not the droppings—was on me. And all were caught in "living color."

Every ornithologist knows this was a significant event. When many young birds reach a certain age and stage of development, they begin to evacuate over the side of the nest, thus keeping it clean. This observation meant the development of this youngster was progressing normally.

Days passed, and eventually I got some images of the juvenile exercising its wings on the nest, which eaglets do to strengthen them in preparation for their first flight. Then I began waiting—and waiting—for it to leave the nest.

One day when the bird was about two and a half months old, I watched through my viewfinder as it climbed onto the far edge of the nest and began furiously beating its wings. Inaudibly I cheered it on, "Go baby, GO!"

But it didn't. It settled back down and went to sleep for the remainder of the day.

I made another visit during the first week of August. As I arrived and set down my gear, Linda Wright stepped out from her hiding place from where she had been watching the nest. She was as frustrated as I was. She had yet to see the eagle fly. "It's been sitting up there on a limb all morning," she reported.

Paul Fournier/Courtesy Maine State Museum

An adult eagle on Swan Island.

I set up my cameras and took several "portraits" of the bird, posing quietly and regally. I moved closer, and the bird suddenly launched out into the air. Flapping easily and surely, it sailed out over the field, circled lazily a couple of times, and then disappeared over a stand of tall pines separating the field from another a quarter-mile beyond. It was over in seconds, but it was magnificent. Both Wright and I were exhilarated.

It was late in August before I could return to Swan Island again. It took only a few minutes to locate the juvenile, perched high up in the pine roosting tree near the nest. It would turn out to be one of the last times I saw this historic young eagle, this eagle that had proven it was possible to transfer viable eagle eggs halfway across the continent to be raised by dedicated and protective foster parents. Following this one success, other transplants were made, and eventually half-grown eaglets, rather than the vulnerable and fragile eggs, were transferred with varying degrees of success.

In the early seventies there were fewer than thirty nesting pairs of eagles in Maine. Now, there are some 350 pairs. Where once there was a lone eagle chick struggling to survive, now there are hundreds. Eagle sightings are once again common in the state. It has been a remarkable comeback for a species that was once thought to be nearing extinction.

Trek to Allagash

In the winter of 1961 a dozen other men and I set off on a 300-mile snowmobile expedition through Maine's remote Allagash region. The junket was the brainchild of Bob Morrill, a northern New England distributor for Polaris Industries, Inc. Polaris manufactured the Sno-Traveler, the modernized "dog team" that was then on the verge of revolutionizing wintertime travel in the North Country. Morrill reasoned that a trek through the last major wilderness stronghold in the East would make a fine test run for some of the company's new experimental models of snowmobiles, not to mention that it would offer up the opportunity to sample the Allagash region's famed trout and togue fishing. Obviously, he had no trouble rounding up a party to go along.

By today's standards, the ten "revolutionary" snow machines we agreed to test were relatively crude. Most had five- to ten-horsepower engines; the largest, I recall, used a sixteen-horsepower Onan engine. For our trip, we had to tow large tote sleds laden with enough food, fuel, and winter camping gear to last thirteen men for a week or more. The larger snowmobiles that we'd use to tow these totes had a unique design: The engine and drive gear were supported on an independently suspended sled with side skis. The theory was that the track could dig down through the deep snow to find solid footing. (The reality would be that they didn't work out that way at all. The track did dig down deep, but it got stuck.) The test sleds also included two lightweight one-person machines, and I was assigned one of those.

Excited to be on our way, we left Millinocket on ten snowmobiles early on a Monday morning, February 26, and headed north toward Baxter State Park. We traveled the first few miles along a delightful woods trail that wound along Millinocket Stream to Millinocket Lake. It was along this trail that the lightweight sled I was driving conked out and refused to start back up. So did the second one-person machine. We pushed them to the side of the trail to be towed out on our way back out. I jumped on the back of one of the other sleds, and would share a ride with other members of the party from then on out.

We crossed Millinocket Lake under a sparkling bright blue sky and were treated to breathtaking views of Mount Katahdin, Maine's highest peak, and its neighbors in the Appalachian Chain. Late that forenoon we reached the entrance to Baxter. Traveling on the park's main roads, which were buried under several feet of snow, we saw the tracks of deer, foxes, rabbits, and moose everywhere, and despite our noisy progress, we also saw several deer themselves. We took a brief lunch break at the Katahdin Stream Campground and pushed on to Sourdnahunk Field Campground for our first overnight stop. We settled into our previously arranged-for bunkhouse there just ahead of a howling snowstorm that moved in at dusk and deposited six inches of new snow during the night.

On Tuesday morning we were under way early. After crossing the ice of six-mile-long Sourdnahunk Lake, we followed logging roads some twenty miles to Telos Lake. From Telos we followed another unplowed logging road about seven miles to the Arm of Chamberlain, where we began our traverse of the upper Allagash's big, sprawling lakes.

I was on the lead snowmobile with Bob Morrill as we started across Chamberlain Lake. Traveling conditions were ideal, and Bob simply headed the machine toward the lake's far end, opened the throttle to cruising speed—perhaps some twenty miles per hour—and we settled back to enjoy the ride. The sensation was amazingly like riding in a boat. Under the new snow, the lake's surface had been formed into long easy "dunes" by the wind, making it feel like swells on the ocean. The snowmobile's toboggan-like snout, plowing through the snow, kicked up a fine "bow spray." We crossed Chamberlain's twenty-two-mile length in slightly over an hour.

At the head of Chamberlain, we crossed over to Eagle Lake via the old "tramway." Fifty years before, when extensive pulp-wood operations were being conducted in the area, a large steam boiler was used here to winch thousands of timber logs between the lakes, which at this point are less than a mile apart. Nearby, the tracks of a backwoods railway once used to haul pulpwood between Eagle and Umbazooksus lakes can still be found, rusting from disuse, and two ancient steam locomotives that rode them are abandoned in the woods. We stopped for a while to examine the rusty relics.

Beyond the tramway we traveled another twenty-odd miles, crossing Eagle Lake, Round Pond, and Churchill Lake, which are connected by thoroughfares. We reached our destination, a cabin near the shore of Heron Lake, late in the after-noon.

The following morning, Wednesday, the group's more avid fishermen headed for the nearby lakes to try the ice-fishing. Others of us used our snowmobiles to explore. Several of us toured the "ghost town" at Churchill Dam, which in its lumbering heyday in the early twentieth century was home to several thousand. Many of the houses remain intact, as do some of the large sheds that housed tools and machinery, including the mammoth Lombard tractors, manufactured in Waterville, Maine. Those ungainly machines, weighing upwards of fourteen tons, hauled long trains of sledges loaded with as many as 125 cords of pulpwood over slickly iced woods roads. One twin-engine job reputedly hauled a 250-cord load.

That afternoon, one of the expeditioners, Paul Doherty, a fellow photography bug, and I decided we'd scoot the fifteen miles to Eagle Lake to check on the ice-fishing activities of two of our comrades, Jack Sevigney and Earlan Campbell. It was snowing and I had to stay crouched down behind the Sno-Traveler's motorcycle-type windshield to keep the wind-whipped flakes from stinging my face. Straddling the seat behind me, Paul was also keeping his head down.

The throttle was nearly three-quarters open, and I was busily staying on top of the controls as I threaded the snowmobile along the shore of the Churchill-Round Pond Thoroughfare. Just a few yards away on our right was thin ice with an occasional patch of open water; to our left was a thick, impenetrable evergreen forest. Hence the circuitous route along the shoreline shelf ice.

We popped onto the broad expanse of Eagle Lake and suddenly Paul shouted, "There they are!"

I had spotted them at about the same instant: a dark object near the lake's far shore, with a couple of tiny figures standing beside it. A minute later I saw snowmobile tracks leaving the main trail. Paul and I leaned into the curve and we tore down the new trail like a train following a trackbed.

As I pulled up near Jack and Earlan—both grinning broadly, we could now see—a ski plane suddenly roared by low overhead, wheeled into a steep bank, and lined up for a landing approach. Paul and I piled off our sled, shouted a quick "Hi" to our two friends, and began hauling out our cameras to snap the approaching plane. We were busy shooting for the next few minutes as the ski plane touched down and taxied up to Jack and Earlan. Two Maine game wardens stepped down from the plane, and after making a routine license check, took off again. They were obviously curious and wanted to keep tabs on us in case of trouble. (They would visit us several more times on the trip.) Paul and I, meanwhile, were ready to see some ice-fishing action, and it wasn't long in coming.

The wardens' plane was barely ten feet off the ground before Jack grabbed an ice skimmer and lit out for the traps at a bouncing jog. Unlimbering my camera and looking around wildly for a flag indicating a bite, I was about to take off running after Jack when Earlan laughed and said, "Relax, there's no flag. That's the way he always travels."

We watched in amusement as Jack bounced up to the first hole, stopped to skim off the newly formed layer of ice, and then resumed jogging until he had cleaned all his holes. Jack had by now established himself as the group's most popular member. In his late fifties, he was the oldest man in the outfit, but he more than made up for his age with bubbling cheerfulness, stamina, and sheer enthusiasm.

Suddenly he tore off again at a dead run. This time we saw there was a flag waving above one of his holes, and the three of us were soon pounding on his heels. A few yards from the hole, he slowed and cautiously approached. Paul and I positioned ourselves with cameras ready as he knelt and peered down into the dark water. Then he looked up at us, eyes shining and face split by a huge grin. "He's on! He's taking out line!" he exulted.

Jack's ice-fishing traps, which he made himself, have a built-on reel mounted on the bottom so that they're always underwater and can't freeze. Now, he gingerly picked up the trap and held it up in the air so we could see the line playing slowly off the reel. Then he carefully laid the trap down beside the hole and held the line loosely in his fingers as it continued to slide steadily down that seemingly bottomless hole.

When the line stopped moving, Jack whispered, "He's following the bait now." For several agonizingly long minutes the line lay dead in Jack's hand. "He'll have that bait down to his tail pretty soon," Earlan muttered. Then the line began moving again.

When the fish stopped again, Jack applied a slight, steady pull on the line. At first, there was no struggle. The line came in steadily, as though there was a dead weight on its end. Yard by painstaking yard, Jack towed the fish in. Earlan picked up the slack line falling from Jack's hand, held it high above the ice so it wouldn't freeze down, and backed away.

Soon the nylon leader came to the surface and the fish stopped. We knew it must be just under the ice. The water bulged in the hole and the line sizzled down again. Jack shouted to Earlan, "Let him have line! Don't snub him!" Earlan, arms held high to keep the line free, ran toward the hole, assuring Jack he'd do as he was told.

Lake trout are not known to be spectacular fighters, and fishing through a hole in the ice with the relatively heavy line and tackle that's required isn't as "sporting" as, say, fly-fishing on a June day using ultralight tackle. We weren't about to witness any smoking fast runs or fantastic splashing, but on this day, the laker's slow deliberate runs and its stubborn hanging back as Jack relentlessly pulled it back each time gradually built up to a high pitch of excitement.

As the fish weakened and the end of the tug-of-war neared, a new element of anxiety entered the picture. The hole had been bored with a Swedish-type ice auger, which makes a hole six inches in diameter. It was now obvious that this fish was too big to come up through that small of a hole. So, while Jack gingerly played the big, struggling fish, Earlan used the auger to bore another hole alongside the first and then broke out the ice between the two holes—a mighty touchy maneuver without cutting the line. But just how big was this fish anyway, and would it fit through the new hole?

Jack settled the issue a few minutes later. After bringing in the line until a couple of feet of the leader was showing, he lowered his arm down into the frigid water nearly to his shoulder. Suddenly, he yanked his arm back up, his fingers hooked inside the gill cover of a nearly three-foot-long trout. A few minutes later, the fish weighed in at nearly ten pounds on Earlan's scale.

Having seen more than we had even hoped to see, Paul and I fired up our Sno-Traveler and began retracing our route back to camp.

Thursday started out bright and sunny but soon gave way to blustery winds and low, racing clouds with intermittently heavy snow squalls. We again spent the day fishing and exploring. A group of us set out late in the afternoon for International Paper Company's large "depot" lumbering camp at Clayton Lake, about twenty miles away, but when we hit fluffy snow

four-feet deep near Umsaskis Lake, with the weather deteriorating, we shortly elected to return to camp.

We left the Heron Lake Camp on the first leg of our journey back "outside" early Friday, which turned out to be the
toughest day, weatherwise, of our trip. Temperatures were in
the 10-below range, and gale-force winds whipped the loose
snow into a swirling ground blizzard, cutting visibility at times
to a few feet. After crossing Churchill and Eagle lakes and part
of Chamberlain in wind-chill conditions of maybe 40- or 50-
below, we stopped at Nugent's Wilderness Sporting Camps,
where it was decided to stay overnight while waiting for conditions to improve.

It should be noted that in those pre–Gore-Tex days, we
were for the most part inadequately dressed for such severe
conditions. Most of us were wearing whatever cold-weather
gear we could find at the Army Surplus Store.

On Saturday the weather was still wild and bitterly cold,
with strong winds and driving snow. We decided to stay holed
up. Al Nugent, the dean of Maine's old-time woodsmen, whose
knowledge of the Allagash region was without peer, gave us a
tour of his camps. "Nuge" and his equally amazing wife, Patty,
with one dollar to their name, moved to Chamberlain Lake in
1936, arriving on a crude raft loaded with all their worldly pos-
sessions. They built a log cabin on the lakeshore and lived off
the land while Nugent trapped furbearers and guided the few
sportsmen who ventured that far. Gradually, he built other cabins and expanded his place into one of the country's unique
wilderness camps.

Everything around the place was handmade, well-built, and
functional. The cabins we stayed in, for instance, had sinks

made from large hollowed-out logs and roofs made of hand-split cedar shakes.

Nugent was a master mechanic and over the years had amassed a staggering variety of machinery and tools. Modern refinements at his camps included a portable sawmill, a monstrous engine-powered log-splitter, electrical power generating plant, and a television set. He also was a master at combining the old and new to achieve his purposes. One fellow in our group spotted a TV antenna, mounted high atop a pole so it could pull in the faraway stations in Bangor. He asked in jest, "Do you have a rotor to adjust the antenna?"

"Sure do," Nugent answered. "I'll show you how it works."

Nearby was a peavey—also called a "cant dog"— a stout-handled tool with a spike and a sharp hook used by lumbermen for rolling heavy logs. Nugent picked it up, took a good "bite" on the pole, and threw his weight against it to twist it.

"How's that line up?" he inquired, eyes a-twinkle.

By Sunday morning the winds had finally let up, but it was snowing heavily as we left Nugent's on the final leg of our return journey to civilization. Following a compass heading, we traveled diagonally across Chamberlain Lake to the Telos Thoroughfare where, following Nugent's directions, we found a woods-hauling road. We encountered deep snow there, and we had to break out a trail using our largest machine. After slightly more than a mile, we were on the main hauling road near Telos Lake.

We retraced our original route to Sourdnahunk Lake and Baxter State Park. The wet, heavy snow that prevailed through the day—measuring over a foot deep in places—hindered our heavily laden sleds on the steep hills, sometimes requiring some pushing and towing to get over them. Nevertheless, that day we traveled nearly seventy miles, all the way from Chamberlain Lake to Baxter's main highway entrance. We ran the last few miles with the aid of headlights after dark in a driving snowstorm. At the park road, we were met by a group of men from Millinocket who were ready with trucks and trailers to haul us and our snow machines back to town.

Later that night we ravenously tore into huge steaks at a Millinocket restaurant. We were one sorry-looking crew—tired, hungry, bearded, and dirty—but we were beaming in the aftermath of our once-in-a-lifetime snowmobile trek. One table over from me I heard Jack Sevigney tell Allen Hetteen, the president of Polaris and the inventor of the Sno-Traveler, "You wait till next year! I've got those Allagash togue figured out now, and I'll really show you fellows how to catch 'em!"

A version of this chapter was first published in *Down East* magazine.

Moose Antics

The lust-minded bull moose emerged from the woods with purposeful stride. Addle-brained and hormonally charged, he circled the plastic deer decoy, sniffing audibly. Then he awkwardly tried to climb aboard and mate with it. In this the moose was somewhat hindered, as the deer decoy barely came up to his knees. Still, he tried a number of times—even after he had knocked the decoy's head off. You never saw a more befuddled-looking moose as he finally gave up and headed reluctantly toward the woods with many a sideways, longing glance back at his unrequited love.

In my many decades of observing moose in Maine, that is only one of numerous weird examples of what they can do when caught up in the madness of the rut. The Native Americans called October the "Mad Moon" because of the way animals behaved during it; maddest of all must have been the largest beast in the Northeast forest, the moose.

Late September and early October make up the moose's mating, or rutting, season. He prepares for it during the summer by building up muscle, fat, and stamina. At the same time his body undergoes other changes. The sockets behind his ears become tender and soon nubbins of antlers begin growing there. When the antlers reach maturity in late summer the blood supply is cut off and they harden, much as a tree dries up and hardens without its nourishing supply of sap.

By then the moose has already felt the first intimation of madness. During his hour of glory, he will be a demoniacal warrior, and as does every good warrior, he tests his weapons. The velvet has been rubbed from his antlers, the broad palms polished and tines sharpened on brush and trees. He stages sham battles with clumps of bushes, and as he grows in confidence (and belligerence), he tackles bigger game. He slams his murderous antlers against full-grown trees, knocking off great slabs of bark and whole limbs and striking terror into the hearts of smaller animals.

When frost whitens the ground the bull moose is ready to venture forth in search of love and combat. By this time a prime male specimen weighs in at about half a ton, carries a lethal set of antlers spanning up to six feet in width, measures better than seven feet at the shoulder, and packs enough wallop in a front hoof to break the back of a full-grown horse. During those few weeks of the rut he is as formidable a creature as roams the continent. And to the cow moose, brute power, noise, and pugnacity are synonymous with sex appeal.

Lust-maddened bulls can be amusing, but they are also unpredictable and potentially dangerous. Plenty of people have reported being charged and chased up trees or whatever by rut-mad bulls. One Maine resident had his parked car, and even his house, repeatedly attacked by a bull. A "good Samaritan" who found a big bull with his antlers entangled and trapped in telephone wire worked long and diligently to get close and cut the wire. The bull thanked him by charging and attempting to gore him.

Every Maine town and city has its local store of moose stories, even Portland, the largest, where almost each year a moose take a stroll through the bustling business district. This usually results in calling out the local police force, game wardens, and biologists, who are led on a merry chase down busy streets and back alleys as they attempt to get close enough to the confused, sometimes panicked, animal to shoot it with a tranquilizer dart and truck it back to the woods. In one such attempt, the darted animal could not be recovered in time and drowned in the harbor.

Moose have ended up in strange places. One young bull entered the capital city of Augusta by crossing a high bridge over the Kennebec River. After snacking in the garden behind the governor's mansion, he gave pursuers a wild chase downtown, even jumping over the hood of a car, before being shot with a tranquilizer and eventually released in the woods a few miles away. Another bull crashed into a septic tank, requiring a crew with a wrecker to raise the smelly animal from its unsavory bath.

The fall rut is the second peak period for moose/vehicle collisions, of which some seven hundred occur annually on Maine's roads, several usually resulting in human fatalities. (The peak period is May to early June when early-growth vegetation and winter's accumulated road salt lure moose; it is also prime time for biting flies, which torment moose unmercifully and drive them out of the woods.)

In a fairly typical encounter, repeated a number of times each fall, a tremendous bull moose was jogging along a highway in northern Maine one September night when he saw a big logging truck bearing down on him. Without a moment's hesitation the bull lowered his massive antlers and charged straight into the glaring headlights. Result: one dead moose, one heavily damaged truck. A year almost to the day after that moose and logging truck tangled, and less than half a mile away, another big bull was prowling along the railroad's right-of-way when a locomotive pulling a string of loaded boxcars came wailing around the bend. Apparently the moose saw it as a monstrous rival. Answering the same blind instinct, he charged down the track straight into the single glaring headlight. I didn't see the result of that encounter, but a trainman later told me: "All we ever found of that big fellow was some hamburg."

A bus carrying students from the little community of Rockwood to the high school in Greenville, twenty-five miles away at the southern tip of Moosehead Lake, was stopped half a dozen times one fall by an aggressive moose. A party of fishermen driving to their camp discreetly followed a large, snorting bull for seven tense miles one night before he finally plunged into the woods and allowed them to pass. Fortunately, the drivers in both those instances were acquainted with moose behavior and knew enough not to antagonize a bull in rut. If they had decided to speed up, crowd the moose, blow the horn, or try to pass, the collision would probably have been a loud one.

One of the most notorious Maine roads for moose collisions is a stretch of U.S. Route 201. It's so notorious, in fact, that it has earned the title of "Moose Alley." Route 201 extends for miles through sparsely populated but moose-riddled territory, from Bingham through Moscow and Jackman to the Canadian border. In hopes of curbing the moose mayhem (which sometimes resulted in four or five crashes per night),

the state sprayed roadside vegetation in known moose-fre-
quented areas with a deer repellent. That didn't work. It then
erected prominent signs bearing moose silhouettes in hopes of
slowing down drivers. Little effect was noted. Finally the state
put up huge signs preceded by rumble strips to grab motorists'
attention, and embedded sensors in the roadway that turn on
powerful blinking lights. Pretty obvious and hard to ignore.
Possibly they prevent some crashes and human injuries and
deaths, but the fact remains that hundreds of the crashes still
happen each year.

While males certainly are the most destructive of the
species, it should be noted that female moose can be far from
docile. A game warden told me about a cow moose that liked
to frequent a swampy area along a highway. The moose was
often visible from the road as she fed on succulent underwater
vegetation. One sunny day a passing motorist spotted the cow
and pulled off on the shoulder for a look-see. This cow—normally the most gentle of creatures—evidently took a disliking
to the intrusion on her privacy. She walked up to the front of
the car, reared up, and struck it with her front hooves.
Repeatedly she reared and struck. She bashed down the hood,
smashed the windshield, and even knocked big holes in the
instrument panel. The warden told me he'd never seen anything like it in a long career in the woods. Why did she do it?
Who knows? Possibly she had a calf nearby and considered the
auto a potential threat. In any case, the car was totaled.
Fortunately, the driver escaped serious injury.

Moose are fun to watch, and every visitor to Maine wants
to see one, but they're wild animals nonetheless, and as such
should be afforded our respect—and our caution.

Crystal Harvest

I look out at a picture-perfect Currier & Ives scene: Across an expanse of frozen lake surface, several burly, bright-garbed men are at work cutting ice with hand saws and chisels. In the background, the wild, forested lakeshore crowds up to a small cluster of log cabins with snow-covered roofs and smoke plumes curling from chimneys.

I'm at Chamberlain Lake in the remote Allagash Wilderness region of Maine to watch the annual rite of putting up the year's supply of ice at Nugent's Wilderness Camps. There are very few places where ice is still cut from pure waters and stored under hay or sawdust until it's dug out again in the warm months and once again used to preserve food, or chill a drink, or retain the freshness of a trout caught for tomorrow's breakfast. Curiosity—and nostalgia—had brought me here.

From the early 1880s into the 1920s, northern ice changed man's centuries-old ways of living throughout much of the world. Ice could efficiently preserve food and provide relief in hot summer climates, and Yankee skippers sailed the globe, peddling this crystal treasure from their homeland of green forests and clean, pure lakes and rivers. Many harvested great wealth from this free "crop" provided by nature in bounteous quantity each winter.

During the heyday of King Ice, the tidewater area of Maine's Kennebec River was the world's center for the booming ice-harvesting industry. The pure Kennebec waters flowing down from Moosehead Lake and its surrounding northern forests, coupled with a rugged winter climate, made the Kennebec the queen of ice rivers. During the 1890s, the average Kennebec ice harvest exceeded three million tons annually, worth over $36 million.

The ice boom employed thousands of able-bodied Mainers, primarily farmers and hired hands from the numerous small farms dotting the river valleys, as well as many itinerant laborers and even hoboes, drawn by the lure of fifteen-cent-an-hour wages and the hearty food and warm beds of riverside boardinghouses.

On those bright, brittle winter days, swarms of men and horses blackened the ice surface as they scraped away the snow, grooved the ice with horse-drawn markers into huge checkerboards, sawed off long strips of the checkered surface, and broke off the individual cakes with heavy iron chisels. Using long poles tipped with steel picks and hooks, other men steered the ice cakes into canals cut through the ice to steam-powered chain-link conveyers. These lifted the heavy cakes into huge icehouses, many larger than football fields, which lined the riverbank. The houses had double walls stuffed with sawdust for insulation.

When the houses were full, the cakes were covered with sawdust or hay to await the arrival of spring. In peak years, the cakes overflowed the houses and the surplus was piled into huge stacks on the riverbank.

Spring meant ice-out, and tall-masted schooners began making their way past Fort Popham at the river's mouth, up the

Kennebec past Bath, through Merrymeeting Bay, and almost to Augusta nearly fifty miles inland. The river's banks were lined with wharves and icehouses, from which the ships would be loaded. Then they caught the earliest favorable tide back downriver to the faraway ports.

Ice was a hot commodity into the twentieth century. Iceboxes were common sights in small towns and villages until late in the 1930s. Refrigerators were sold in stores, but not many families could afford such a luxury in those Great Depression days. As a very young child, I remember seeing the horse-drawn ice wagon, pulled by a large, gentle chestnut, working the streets and making deliveries in my hometown. Later, the horse and wagon were replaced by a more efficient, but less picturesque, stake-body truck. When I got old enough, I sometimes joined neighborhood boys in chasing after the truck to "steal" chips from its tailgate. The driver purposely looked the other way while we stealthily gathered the chips; he'd made sure they were lying on the tailgate for us.

I remember my dad dropping chunks of ice into a burlap bag and using the back of his ax to crush the ice into smaller pieces. These were then dumped, along with some rock salt, into the ice-cream maker, which already contained ingredients from Mom. We bigger boys fought to turn the hand crank for the seemingly interminable length of time it took it to turn hard, indicating the ice cream was finished. Then the luckiest kid—if not the biggest—got the chance to lick the frozen cream off the paddle, which was so cold your tongue some-times stuck to it. Nothing since has ever tasted as good.

Ice harvesting in the North Country remained a necessity long after the availability of refrigerators. If a remote sporting

Paul Fournier/Courtesy Maine State Museum

Ice harvesting at Nugent's.

camp didn't have access to electricity to run a refrigerator, what good was it?

The annual ice harvest at Nugent's Camps on Chamberlain Lake took place on a March day sparkling bright with frost. Fortified with one of Patty Nugent's lumberjack breakfasts, we gathered on the ice to watch Al Nugent and his three-man crew at work.

Al Nugent was a big man, a man of legendary size and strength. In his early years at Chamberlain he did the entire ice-cutting job alone, spending weeks at the harsh labor. "I'd saw out the cakes, load 'em on a moose sled, and haul them by hand up t' the icehouse," he recalled.

One story of his great strength we heard from someone else. Several ice fishermen had gathered around to watch Nugent at work. Each tried his strength at lifting one big cake from the water, but failed. One of the men bet Nugent that he couldn't single-handedly lift the cake a foot clear of the ground. Nugent took the challenge, spat on his hands, grabbed the ice tongs, grinned, hoisted the cake high, and almost trotted with it all the way up to the icehouse without setting it down once to rest. (Nugent had built the icehouse himself, by the way, from hand-hewn logs. The roof was made of hand-split cedar shakes.)

Nugent had made a few concessions to age and modern times at this particular ice harvest. While he used his tractor blade to plow the snow cover off a selected area of ice, his wife's nephew, Lee, Nugent's right-hand man, was in the woods cutting four small evergreen trees to use to mark the corners of the ice field. Chamberlain's icy surface serves as a highway for snowmobiles and a landing strip for light planes, and the tree markers would warn of thin ice if the hole should refreeze and be covered with snow.

Lakes seldom freeze the same way from one season to another. During "open" winters with light snowfall, the ice freezes hard, blue, and thick as the cold penetrates deep. Early heavy snowfalls, on the other hand, insulate the water from the cold air so the ice cover can remain thin and hazardous to travel regardless of the cold.

This winter had started off cold and open so that a two-foot layer of hard blue ice formed in December and January. Then heavy snow, followed by winter rains, blanketed the lake in February and pressed down on the ice, causing it to crack and allowing lake water to seep up into the snow. This created for several weeks an ice traveler's nightmare: deep slush.

When Nugent chiseled a hole though one corner of his field for the ice saws, he discovered a problem. A subzero cold snap in early March had penetrated deep into the slush layer, freezing it into a foot of "snow-ice." Beneath that was a six-inch layer of water and then solid blue ice two feet thick beneath it all. Nugent had seen about every ice condition. "Snow-ice keeps about as good as blue ice and it works just as well in the icebox," he said, grinning at us. He decided to harvest the snow-ice as well as the blue, but the separate layers meant that each would have to be sawed separately.

One of the remaining two crew members, burly paper mill workers from Millinocket, used a straight board to mark off the cutting field and to mark saw lines about one foot apart. Then, a chain saw was used to score along the lines and relieve—by just a bit—the amount of hand-sawing that would have to be done.

The crew took turns sawing along the lines and cutting the ice field up into approximate one-foot-wide strips. A heavy, toothed "busting bar" was used to break up the strips into individual blocks that could be easily handled by one man.

As the blocks floated free, Nugent pulled them out of the water with large ice tongs and loaded them aboard his tractor sledge. By late forenoon, the first sledge-load of ice began its trip to the icehouse, where the thick log walls and a cover of sawdust would keep it frozen.

After lunch, the toughest work began. The ice field, with its snow-ice removed, now looked like a swimming pool for the Polar Bear Club. But invisible under that water was a two-foot-thick layer of blue ice. Enter the freshly filed ice saws, teeth gleaming. Two sawyers set out to nibble their way around the big square hole, advancing a mere inch or so with each saw stroke.

All hands, including yours truly, took turns manning the heavy saws. The technique is simple and direct: the cutting is done on the downstroke because the teeth are pointed downward. Hand-sawing, whether it be cutting ice or cutting wood, forces patience upon the sawyer by its very nature. There's just no way to speed up the process. Try to hurry the saw along and you merely waste energy because the saw kerf, or cut, jams with ice chips and the teeth run off at angles from the path of the cut. No self-respecting sawyer wants to leave a telltale crooked kerf. Straight cuts save labor and, as Nugent pointed out, square-cut cakes pack more tightly for better keeping in the icehouse.

Among those watching the harvest was Harry Crooker, a friend of mine and the Nugents. He was born and raised on the shores of Merrymeeting Bay on the lower Kennebec River. Not only had he witnessed the last few years of commercial ice there, as a boy he had also worked on the Kennebec ice fields with his father. Old-time sawyers on the Kennebec, he said, cut with a circular motion, holding the saw away from the body on the upstroke. "This lets the blade slide back away from the cut, and allows the loosest chips to float clear. Keeps the blade from binding and sticking," he said. We all tried it and unanimously agreed that professional ice sawing requires a lot of preconditioning. It also must be a helluva great way to develop chest, arm, and shoulder muscles.

Gradually, like a great, blue, harpooned whale, the massive ice block rose. One end thrust up into the air, streaming water, and then settled back as the ice floe sought equilibrium and leveled itself.

Then the sawing began anew as the big ice block—Nugent estimated it weighed several tons—was cut into cakes that were hauled up onto the ice, glistening cold-blue in the bright afternoon sun.

While the others sawed, Nugent loaded his sledge and made repeated trips up the snowy trail to the icehouse, where nephew Lee was working feverishly, stacking ice cakes in tightly packed layers. He shoved snow between each layer, tamping it down in cracks to fill any holes. If left unfilled, the holes could lead to melting.

After Lee had packed several loads, he and others called it a day, and they succumbed to one of Patty's great repasts and a social evening around the cozy camp stove.

The next morning found all hands back on the ice under lowering skies and spitting snow. A thin ice shell had skimmed the open water overnight, but it soon disappeared as the saws and chisels and busting bars were put to work on the slowly diminishing ice block.

By noontime, several more loads of blue ice had been hauled ashore. The final load was put away in the later afternoon. In a few days, Nugent and Lee would get around to covering the ice with an insulating layer of sawdust. There was no danger of its melting in this Allagash climate for at least a few more weeks.

The put-up ice would last Nugent all year, until it was time again for the annual harvesting rite.

Return of the Caribou

I t all began for me on a late-winter day in 1986. Glenn
Manuel, who was then the commissioner of the Maine
Department of Inland Fisheries and Wildlife, invited me
to a meeting in his Augusta office. There I met an old acquaintance and made a new one. The former, Francis Dunn, a part-
time real estate agent in the small northern Maine community
of Patten, had recently retired after three decades as a wildlife
biologist for the department. The other gentleman at the meeting was Ladd Heldenbrand, a businessman from the Portland
area and, not insignificantly, a retired doctor of veterinary
medicine.

Manuel laid a miniature bombshell on me when, with a
mischievous look, he inquired: "How would you like to be
involved in a project to bring caribou back to Maine?"

Ah, that's why Dunn and Heldenbrand were there. I
remembered that they had been involved in an ill-starred
attempt to restore caribou to Maine in 1963.

I had questions. Where would the caribou come from?
Where would they be released? How would such a costly project be funded? It was estimated that $100,000 a year for at
least five years would be needed. And, having failed a quarter
of a century ago, why would it work now? Some of the
answers—funding, for one—were not forthcoming for many

months. As this is written, years later, some are still unanswered.

I signed on for the project, not knowing what problems lay
ahead: short funding, history-making storms, a silent caribou-
killer that would undo all the best efforts, and even attacks
from a sector of the public and media that would attempt to
scuttle the whole project.

In the weeks and months following that first meeting, the
evolution of the project grew slowly and in fits and starts. It
soon became clear that the Maine Department of Inland
Fisheries and Wildlife, despite Manuel's enthusiastic support,
would not be able to underwrite any of the costs, nor commit
state resources to the project. The department was just emerging from a nightmare two-year battle for its fiscal life in the
Maine State Legislature, and with all of the resulting wounds
still fresh and oozing blood, it was obvious that a caribou rein-
troduction program would have to be a nonpolitical, self-sup-
porting private effort.

Thus was formed the nonprofit Maine Caribou Transplant
Committee. Manuel became its first chairman, with Francis
Dunn and Ladd Heldenbrand among its charter members. As
interest and excitement began to grow, so did the number of
supporters. Donations began trickling in. Many Mainers,
whose fathers and grandfathers had told them stories of seeing
caribou in the Maine woods during their youth, were thrilled
at the prospect of being able to see them themselves.

But there were doubters and detractors, too. Among the
most vociferous was a group who suspected the project was
intended only to build up a herd of easy-to-kill targets for
bloodlusting hunters. That the commissioner of Fisheries and
Wildlife, with its large supportive base of sportsmen, was the

project chairman was offered as proof otherwise, along with the fact that it was said from the outset the aim was never to permit caribou hunting in Maine, but the opposition persisted.

Meanwhile, after screening many applicants, the committee unanimously selected Dr. Mark McCollough as project director. McCollough, a University of Maine wildlife biology graduate, worked for Fish and Wildlife in nongame and endangered species programs.

More headway was made. Folks in Newfoundland, which had been identified as the nearest possible source of caribou, were receptive and enthusiastic about the project. In June, then governor John Brennan officially presented the idea to Newfoundland premier Brian Peckford, and soon after, the two political leaders announced an agreement.

Canadian wildlife biologists Eugene Mercer and Shane Mahoney would assist in the project. They and their colleagues had spent years intensively studying and experimenting with the island's caribou population. (Evidently their work was a considerable success, as the herd had grown by 13 percent annually for some years.) They had literally lived out on the barrens with the caribou, studying how they lived, what they preferred to eat, who their enemies were. At the time, they had successfully translocated herds of caribou twenty-three out of twenty-four times.

That August, Mercer and Mahoney flew to Maine to look over potential release sites and to share their expertise with the committee. Among that expertise was a way to prevent the project from failing as its 1963 counterpart had. The Canadians pointed out the fact that back then, the caribou had been immediately released in Maine upon their arrival. There was no attempt to hold them on-site for a period of acclimatization or familiarization. The caribou disappeared, they said, because, no doubt following their ingrained natural instincts, they had simply tried to migrate back to their summer range when spring returned, not knowing that that summer range was 1,000-plus miles and a sea journey away.

Instead, the Canadians said, the plan, which had worked successfully in Canada, would be to hold the transplanted caribou in a relatively confined area for several years, allowing them to breed and produce a new group of offspring. These newborns, with no inherent herd "memory" of their parents' homeland, would become imprinted with their birthplace. In two or three years, when the young became mature enough to fend on their own, they would be the first to be liberated. In theory, at least, any migratory urges they might develop would bring them right back to this same "home" place. Later, after five or six years of producing new crops of offspring, all of the caribou—including those that still survived from the original parent group—would be released in the same place. By then, it was theorized, any residual instinct to migrate in the parents would, hopefully, be muted by their desire to remain with the rest of the herd.

Mercer and Mahoney also offered up an irresistible ace: They knew of a sedentary, nonmigratory herd on the Avalon Peninsula in southeast Newfoundland. Members of that herd were free for the taking, provided Americans paid for the costs of capture and transport.

Wheels were set in motion. A five-acre area at the University of Maine in Orono was selected as the "holding area" for the caribou; here they would go through the imprinting phase. The university's Wildlife Division would provide a pool of experienced large-mammal biologists and veterinarians, as well as students and graduate students eager to volunteer their services, to look after the care and feeding of the caribou. When the caribou were ready, they would be released in the wild at a site to be chosen later. The committee was eyeing Mount Katahdin in Baxter Park, which offered the best conditions in the state. For one thing, the park harbors few deer, which carry *P. tenuis*, a parasite that causes brainworm in caribou. For another, the park is a 200,000-acre preserve with limited and controlled access—and no hunting is permitted.

Early on, the caribou capture had been scheduled for early fall, prior to the stressful mating period, or "rut." But as autumn approached, the target date became unrealistic. The holding pens in Orono weren't ready. An October capture would interfere with Canadian hunting seasons. And, most critical of all, the committee still didn't have sufficient funds to pull it off. An early-December date was substituted as more realistic, allowing more time to beat the bushes for contributions. (And as Mahoney also pointed out, a December capture would be a better bargain for the thrifty Yankees. Since up to 90 percent of adult female caribou become pregnant each fall, the Mainers could bring home almost two caribou for the price of one.)

Throughout the summer of 1986, anticipation and planning for the project had grown feverishly, but not so the coffers. Despite a round of dinners for wealthy members of Portland high society and other fund-raising schemes, donations continued to just trickle in. There was the occasional contribution of several thousand dollars, but most were on the order of smaller donations from schoolchildren, sportsmen's clubs, and similar small organizations—just enough to keep bailing the committee out and pay the bills, but far from the enormous costs the project would ring up.

Former Maine governor Horace H. Hildreth of Bangor saved the day. Hildreth had been following the project—and the fund-raising—with great interest. As head of a successful family, the eighty-year-old decided to contribute $50,000. In a letter to the caribou fund he wrote:

> *. . . In making this gift, I have two thoughts in mind. In the first place, the people of Maine were kind enough to elect me to two terms as their Governor, and I have long had in mind some sort of a gift to express my appreciation for the privilege they conferred upon me. In the second place, I have long felt it was most unfortunate that a previous attempt to reestablish caribou in the State of Maine failed, and that another attempt deserved support.*

The project could go on.

Meanwhile, reporters—from the major television networks and newswire services, regional and local broadcasts, magazines, international and local newspapers—were beseeching me and my media coordinator counterpart in Canada, Robert Greenwood, then public information assistant to the minister of the Newfoundland Department of Culture and Recreation, for information. The demands made by some were incredibly arrogant and rude. Each wanted some advantage over the rest of the field, some exclusive—and preferably sensational or scandalous—piece of information with which to scoop the competition. One TV station sent its crew up to Newfoundland early in the fall, hoping to get the jump, but they blew their budget, and were unable to go back up and cover the actual, newsy portion of the captures. One major U.S. network, unable to be assured of exclusivity in the use of a helicopter, chose not to cover the event at all.

The phone lines were kept busy between Augusta and St. John's, as Greenwood and I tried to plot strategy for containing these ravening beasts of the press. One advantage we had was that the caribou would be captured and processed for the trip to Maine on government-owned property, where rules had to be followed. Noncompliance could and would be dealt with by removing the offenders forcibly from the property. Press guidelines were prepared and issued to all media planning to attend.

The Canadians had been most adamant in controlling the use of helicopters, mandating that only one media-pool helicopter be permitted to chase or follow each of the two capture helicopters. Reporters and producers howled loudly at that, but the authorities stuck to their guns in the interests of safety and fairness to all the media representatives.

We were getting closer, but one nagging question remained unanswered until late in the game: How would the thirty caribou, once tranquilized and captured, be transported to Maine? Another rescuer appeared: Merrill Transport Company of Portland, one of the state's largest and oldest trucking firms, offered to haul the caribou. They were joined by Wormell Farms of Portland, which offered the use of a big, specially designed cattle-hauling trailer.

Merrill awarded two of its top throttle-jockeys the task of driving the big, shined-up rig to Newfoundland and back. For veteran Herman LaBelle, a rather roly-poly, jolly-faced, happy Mainer from Cape Elizabeth, this would be his final trip for Merrill prior to his retirement. Joining him would be Jim White, a young, tall, quiet man who had recently been presented the company's safe driver award. There would be times when the drivers would question the merits of receiving this "honor."

The Capture

Finally, December was at hand. All preparations had been made and it was time to go get the caribou. Project director McCollough and I made the three-day road trip to St. John's together. December 3, 1986, dawned clear and cold in St. John's, a perfect day to be introduced to the caribou of the Avalon Peninsula. One of my tasks during the capture and transfer project would be to film the operation on videotape, both to provide video footage to news broadcasters and, eventually, to complete a video documentary for use in fund-raising. It was essential that I obtain scenes of the Avalon caribou in their pristine home environment and, to that end, I'd arranged a meeting with one of Newfoundland's best and most experienced caribou experts, Con Finlay, a wildlife biologist for the Newfoundland Wildlife Division. In order to meet him I had to make a two-hour drive down the Avalon Peninsula to Trepassey, a small fishing village. We became acquainted over a steaming cup of coffee at an otherwise-deserted cafe at the edge of town.

I had expected to be flown in by helicopter to some remote area of the peninsula in order to get close enough to film the caribou in their habitat, but not so. Finlay assured me he'd have me in sight of caribou within the hour, and only a few miles away. We finished our coffee and headed out of town. We topped out on the open barrens: not a tree for as far as the eye could see in any direction. It was a flat, gently rolling, snowy landscape not unlike the winter plains of western Kansas. We drove east possibly ten miles, seeing nothing. We were approaching a power line and road heading south to St. Shott's, the small fishing village located at the very southern tip of the Avalon, when Finlay made a sort of grunting sound, and pointed to the right.

Even though I strained my eyes, I couldn't see them for a couple of minutes. A high, thin layer of clouds obscured the sun, making for a flat and suffused light that, while ideal for photography, reduced contrast and made it hard to pick out specific objects. Then a movement caught my eye, and a small group of a half-dozen caribou cows and their calves came into focus. No wonder I hadn't been able to see them. I'd been looking for the brownish-buff caribou I'd seen in photographs, but that is their summer coloration. Now they were wearing their predominantly whitish winter coats. Their winter coloration allows the caribou to blend almost perfectly with their snowy background—a fact that would become abundantly and frustratingly clear when we began searching for them by helicopter.

I began spotting small scattered groups of caribou. There was no great endless herd as seen in documentaries of the barren-ground caribou of northern Labrador and Quebec, but there were plenty for my photo purposes. The caribou drifted slowly, with single-minded purpose. They stopped frequently to paw down through the thin snow cover for a tasty biteful of shrub or lichens. They ignored us unless we got too close— 100 or 200 feet. Then they would slow-trot off 200 or 300 yards and resume their leisured pace.

That evening before dinner back in St. John's I was able to hook a videotape recorder up to the television set in our room and show Mark McCollough his first close-up view of the Avalon caribou we'd driven so far to find.

Thursday was the first scheduled day of captures, but a storm weathered us in for the day. On Friday, McCollough and

I left early for the capture site on the grounds of the Salmonier Correctional Center near St. Joseph, about an hour's drive from St. John's. It was deceptively quiet at the site at that early dawn hour, but there was an air of tension. The capture crew was already on-site, dressed in heavy parkas and muskrat-fur caps with big, thick leather mittens reaching nearly to the elbow, each with a wool-fleece patch on the back of the hand ("to warm your nose on when it's cold," Con Finlay told me). They looked prepared for any weather Newfoundland could dish out.

The capture field, an area of perhaps ten acres, had been carefully prepared for our project. Behind a hump at the north end of the clearing were about a dozen red and orange steel drums and hand pumps, ready for refueling the choppers. At the midpoint of the field sat the two capture helicopters—Bell 407 Long Ranger, capable of carrying the pilot and one passenger in the front, separated from the passenger/cargo bay by a bulkhead. There were four bare-metal seats in the passenger bay. All nonessential equipment had been stripped out—including seat pads and backrests—to save every possible extraneous ounce of weight. Near the helicopter landing spot, a heavy-duty weighing scale with a large hook hung underneath a log A-frame. There also was a warming hut and a small shed for use by the wildlife technicians.

I watched as, inside the shed, the technicians carefully loaded syringes with the tranquilizer drug, M-99, and placed them into metal toolboxes. There was no joking around. We had heard stories about this particular drug. Scary stories. It was said to be lethal within minutes to humans, even in minute amounts, such as from an accidental prick or scratch of the skin. The only remedy was an antidote that each shooter would carry with him, which must be administered immediately. (I heard one story of a veterinarian who, while injecting an animal, accidentally stuck himself with the needle. He was found the next room over, lying dead on the floor, his outstretched hand holding the key with which he was about to unlock the cabinet containing the antidote. True? I don't know.) I resolved then and there to be very careful and look first before I sat down in the helicopter.

Finally, the pilots climbed aboard; the rotor blades began turning, slowly at first and gathering momentum as the engines whined up. It was time to get started. The crews climbed aboard, the choppers lifted and whump-whumped off to the southeast. The rest of us waited. I'd been itching to go on this first trip out, but was told I'd have a seat on the second. The caribou were supposedly close by; it was anticipated we'd have our quota of twenty-seven females and three stags by midday of the second day.

An hour went by before the first helicopter reported that it was on its way back in with a caribou. A forest of lenses and microphones followed the arrival of the Long Ranger as it swept in low over the trees, dropped down, hovered several feet over the ground, and swung around to bring the loading door in line with the weighing station before gently settling in. A half-dozen people ducked under the rotor blades and approached the door. Within minutes they slid the doe out and onto a plywood pallet, which they carried to the weighing site. Camera shutters clicked and motor-drives whirred as countless photos were taken of this historic first capture for the Maine Caribou Transplant.

The center of all this attention was a smallish doe whose nose quivered from the drug's effects. She was weighed and measured and then, minutes after arriving, was loaded aboard a pickup truck and sent on her way down to the cattle truck, where veterinarians Ladd Heldenbrand and Doug Tweedie and a coterie of other vets and aides waited. As she was driven away, all eyes and cameras turned to the second helicopter, just arriving with caribou No. 2.

Now it was my turn to board a helicopter, joining Finlay, Mahoney, and the rest of the crew. We lifted up to some 700 to 800 feet, offering us a good view of the Avalon Peninsula terrain—or what I could see of it from my aft-facing position. Several times, one or another of the crewmen with a better view would point out a moose, appearing near-black against the snow below. Soon the snow began to break up into patches interspersed by bare ground and we began seeing caribou— small, isolated bunches at first. At our approach, they began running, darting sideways and sometimes doubling back under us. They are much more agile than they appear when browsing at leisure.

The pilot selected a larger caribou herd and dropped down to within thirty or forty feet above the ground. In seconds we overtook the herd and I saw flashes of white bodies darting past the window, exploding in all directions. Mahoney, the tranquilizer shooter, was unable to lock in on an individual long enough to get off a shot. We went down again, over another herd. I honestly don't know how long we kept this up as a strong wind buffeted us about. The caribou obviously were doing all they could to keep away from us. At last, Mahoney fired and hit a doe in the lower rear leg.

It takes seven to ten minutes for the tranquilizer to take effect. Go down close too soon, and you stimulate the animal, possibly minimizing the tranquilizer's effect. Stay too far away,

A helicopter overtakes a caribou herd near St. Joseph, Newfoundland.

and the caribou could disappear in a clump of woods and be
lost from view. So we hovered, watched her, and waited. At
one point, pilot Joe Powers observed over the intercom, to no
one in particular as far as I could tell: "I'm having to fly into
this wind at fifty to sixty knots, just to hold station." The
chopper bucked and bounced; it was damned windy!

Finally, the caribou was lying down and still. Mahoney
spoke into his mouthpiece: "All right. Let's go down after her."

It had been agreed earlier that, if possible, without interfer-
ing with the operation, the helicopter would first let me off,
then climb up a short distance while I set myself up behind the
animal to get the shot of the helicopter settling down again
with the caribou in the foreground. (That's showbiz, folks.)
Mahoney gave me the go-ahead nod.

The last thing I wanted to do was embarrass myself in front
of these guys. It was important for me to project a Joe Cool

image. So you know I blew it. Powers landed the helicopter and I hopped out onto the tundra, shouldering my heavy camera and tape deck. At my second step I was momentarily stopped up short . . . then the headphones peeled off my ears and slapped back on their coiled cord, bouncing off the floor of the chopper. I caught a momentary glimpse of Con Finlay's smiling visage before I ducked under the rotor blades and started for the caribou. Me, excited? Nah!

What had appeared from the air to be smooth tundra was something else up close. I scrambled over ledge, loose rocks, low brush, and slippery moss with my heavy load, puffing and sweaty by the time I reached the caribou. She was breathing normally, head up and quivering slightly from the drug, and she was apparently oblivious to my close presence. I got down on my knees for steadiness, focused the caribou at the bottom of the picture frame, and raised my arm to give the helicopter the high sign to come in. As it descended, I could hear the press chopper approaching and then off to my right.

Within minutes, Mahoney and his crew were at the caribou's side. The dart was removed from the hind leg, wiped off on Shane's trouser leg, and stuffed into a jacket pocket. (I recall wondering if he wasn't being a bit cavalier in his handling of this syringe dart, which a few minutes ago had been loaded with a potentially lethal drug.) A folding aluminum stretcher was opened up and laid beside the caribou. Con Finlay used a long piece of stout rope to securely tie her legs together, just like I've seen rodeo cowboys truss up a roped cow. A creamy substance was squeezed from a tube onto her eyeballs to keep them moist until she woke up. She was carefully rolled onto the stretcher and secured in place with a rugged canvas belt around her belly. Evidently, these fellows were placing a high

Paul Fournier/Courtesy Maine State Museum
The caribou flee from the hovering helicopter.

priority on not having her come loose on the way back. An
unexpectedly roused caribou in a helicopter could wreak havoc
and inflict serious injuries—something to be avoided. The men
picked up the litter and carried her back to the idling helicopter.

With the crew in the back compartment with the caribou, I rode up front with the pilot and took in the great rolling plateau of Avalon from the bubble-windowed nose of the helicopter. The landscape, made up primarily of low, ground-hugging bushes and heaths, was littered by hundreds of automobile-sized rocks (called "erratics"), left there 10,000 years ago by retreating glaciers. Pockets of spruce and fir hugged low depressions where they could escape the battering winds.

As we moved north, we approached an area of small mountains—rocky upthrusts rising several hundred feet. At about this point, we also encountered a heavy snow squall, which closed in around us with lightning speed and reduced visibility to a few hundred feet. But pilot Powers obviously knew the terrain intimately. He threaded his way past the hills, with their menacing rocky cliffs, without hesitation.

We moved past the snow shower and had the Salmonier landing field in sight. Soon we settled down before the cannon-like lenses of the press gallery. Within minutes, our caribou was unloaded, and we were in the air again. The other capture chopper had also delivered a caribou, and with four females in the truck, Mahoney decided it was time to go after a mature male. Handling a big male would require both crews, so the second capture helicopter followed us as well.

With the caribou area now located, we lost no time returning to it, and it wasn't long before Powers had us chasing caribou again. Our adrenaline surged. Finlay, the shooter this time, was the picture of a Western movie star, scanning the roadside for bandits from the stagecoach, as he watched for a shooting opportunity. When it came, he proved as deadly at the game as

Mahoney. His first shot hit the big stag high on the rump. A perfect hit.

Again, there was the wait for the animal to stagger to a halt and drop. Again, we settled down nearby to allow me to alight for the showbiz shot. Just as I was about to open the door, Finlay's voice boomed out: "Don't forget to remove your headphones, Paul!" And the cabin erupted in guffaws.

The caribou I approached on the ground was a magnificent male with a classic set of huge antlers. Helicopters were settling in all around me—the other capture crew to assist and the two media craft—as I prepared to film our chopper re-descending behind the stag in the foreground. It was a setting worthy of *Wild Kingdom*.

Handling the big stag took all the muscle of both crews. The procedure was the same as with the cows, but slower and more difficult. The soundtrack of the video I recorded of it carries every panting breath, grunt, and oath picked up by Mahoney's radio-microphone.

With the big fellow on board, there was definitely no chance for me to ride back in that helicopter, so I climbed into the other capture chopper with Dave Slade as the designated shooter.

We were in the thick of the caribou range now, and it wasn't long before we were chasing a herd. Within minutes, Slade took a sighting, fired, and scored another dead hit. These guys were incredible. I'd witnessed three shots without a miss.

This time, our caribou, a female, dropped within a small circle of stunted spruce trees near a small pond. With a couple of captures and loadings already filmed, we wasted little time for showbiz setups. We shortly had her loaded aboard, and were on our merry way back to Salmonier and the waiting press corps.

This high-adventure portion of the captures ended too soon for me. I'd enjoyed the chases, the adrenaline rush, the camaraderie. Now, I was once again a mere spectator. I drifted down to the cattle trailer, where doctors McCollough, Heldenbrand, and Tweedie and a cadre of other vets and helpers were "processing" a caribou. Efficiently, with assured skills, they injected her with antibiotics and anti-parasite medications; clipped numbered tags to her ears; removed a tooth for aging; and took blood samples. One fellow, wearing surgical gloves, had the unpleasant task of retrieving a fecal sample from her rectum, which he accomplished with swift, sure ease. (Blood and fecal samples were shipped by air daily to a federal government laboratory at Sackville, New Brunswick, to analyze for parasites.) Then the caribou was carried in to a small fenced-off area inside the rear of the trailer. A quick injection of antidote, and she was, amazingly to me, struggling to her feet within seconds. A few staggered steps, and she was ready to be let out into the main portion of the trailer, where she immediately melted in with the other caribou.

After there were eleven caribou in the trailer, the Maine delegation held a consultation outside near the tailgate. The topic: the male caribou—more precisely, their antlers.

"We've got to remove those antlers," someone insisted. "They're too aggressive against the females. They could hurt them. Might even kill them."

Prior to leaving Maine, we had been told the cattle trailer would be divided into several small pens so the animals could be kept apart in small, manageable groups, with the males segregated. That had not been done, and it was not feasible to make the change now. The antlers had to come off.

Within a few minutes' time, the stags were tranquilized and their antlers were removed with a hacksaw. The effect was amazing. With their male regalia gone, the stags reverted to meek docility. There were no more charges or attacks in the trailer.

Day Two began a bit less stressful than the first. With most of the media gone, the crew could concentrate more fully on the task at hand. But the weather was deteriorating. Snow showers were becoming more frequent—and heavier—as the day progressed. That this was hampering the captures was evident in the slow pace in which the helicopters were returning with their live cargoes. As the day wore on, it got worse. The squalls, sometimes more sleet or ice pellets than snow, were unrelenting, and by late afternoon it became obvious that we would not have anywhere near our quota of thirty caribou that day. We ended the day with twenty-three on board the truck—three stags and twenty does. We'd intended to spend the next day, Sunday, driving down the island and catching the ferry back to Nova Scotia Sunday night or Monday morning, but we had to revise those plans. We'd have to spend a part of Sunday, at least, rounding out our catch of animals.

On Sunday morning we drove back out to the site through falling snow. There was no letup. At times the snow was heavy enough that I was sure the choppers could only set down and wait for it to ease. How could they find caribou in this weather? At any other time, reason would have dictated that we lay over for the day and wait for improved conditions. But there were extenuating pressures: The caribou from the first day's capture had now been aboard the trailer a long time and still faced the ordeal of a long ride to Maine. They could not survive many days of such confinement. We didn't have the luxury of time to take the day off.

In order to try to expedite matters, the two helicopters used by the media the first two days were pressed into service. They would follow the capture choppers and, when a caribou was downed, they'd pick it up and ferry it back to base, allowing the capture crew to remain and pursue another animal and thus save the lengthy and unproductive ferrying time.

This was helpful, but still not enough, given the near-impossible conditions. By late afternoon, a decision had been

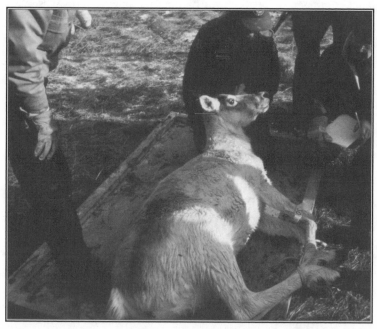

Paul Fournier/Courtesy Maine State Museum

A doe is "processed" at Salmonier, including being injected with antibiotics and anti-parasite medications, before being taken to the trailer for transport to Maine.

made. We had to move out with the caribou we had—three males and twenty-four females. It would mean driving with them all night in order to meet the daily ferry at Channel-Port aux Basques the next day. The trailer was hitched up to the tractor, and all the necessary gear loaded aboard in preparation for the trip home. The caribou were given fresh water and a substantial supply of food, with several pickup truckloads of fresh lichens and moss. One of the Newfoundland crew told me: "We sure had a helluva time findin' and pickin' all that moss from under the snow!"

The Odyssey

And so, on the evening of December 8, 1986, the Newfoundland-to-Maine Caribou Caravan began its odyssey. The Merrill Transport truck, pulling its light but precious cargo, led the way. We followed, in our heavy-laden little station wagon.

On the way up from Maine, McCollough and I, with our paraphernalia, including all the video gear, had pretty much filled up the Chevy Celebrity station wagon. Or so we thought. Now, homeward bound, we had another passenger: Ladd Heldenbrand—to say nothing of all his medicine bags and kits. Half the backseat and all of the luggage compartment were taken up with bags and cases. There was barely enough room for us three humans. My six-foot, 180-pound hulk didn't help the situation. Comfortable seating arrangements would turn out to be the least of our worries on the drive.

We began the 600-plus-mile journey across the island of Newfoundland under reasonably dry road conditions. Traffic was extremely light; as the evening wore on, we would drive for miles with only the taillights of the caribou trailer leading the way. We stayed far enough behind so as not to bother the caribou with our headlights.

We had covered perhaps a hundred miles when the first friendly Newfoundland snowflakes began to reappear, very light and scattered at first, blown about by a skittish wind. It was an ominous beginning for anyone who is familiar with snow country; the worst storms always start lightly. The snow started to come down in rather serious fashion by the time we reached our first refueling stop near Gander Airport. Visibility was worsening. There was no sign of a snowplow; evidently Canadians do not waste energy plowing at night. Other motorists were obviously aware of this and were holed up somewhere, because we had the road to ourselves. We also were becoming concerned about another hazard: We had already seen several moose standing on the edge of the road. If one happened to be standing in the travel lane, we'd never spot it through the falling snow in time to stop or avoid it. We knew what sort of damage a collision with a 1,000-pound moose could do to our small car—and to us. There was no relaxing at the wheel.

We had no way of knowing it, but we were committed on a collision course with one of the most violent winter storms along the northeast American and maritime coasts in years. It was gathering power and strength in the Gulf of Maine, being fueled by cold air from the land clashing with warmer air from over the Atlantic Ocean. By the time it would explode over the Gulf of St. Lawrence in some twenty-four hours, it would be packing the power of nuclear bombs. And we'd be there to meet it.

The middle part of our trip to Channel-Port aux Basques is lost to my memory in a blur of swirling white, burning eyes, and stiff back and neck muscles. The driving situation was aggravated by our heavy load. With the car squatted down at the rear, our headlights were pointed upwards, into the blinding-white curtain of snow. It formed an impenetrable, reflective traveling wall, possibly thirty feet ahead of us. We couldn't see the caribou truck, but its trail of tire tracks was our salvation. As long as we could see those, we knew we were okay. Fighting the storm, we drove on, and on.

A few hours and many miles later a faint dawn light began to suffuse the world. Our field of vision began expanding beyond the curtain of white that had preceded us all night long. We looked out at a wind-lashed, gray-white world. We hadn't seen a single snowplow or sand truck during that entire long night.

At a point perhaps about twenty-five to thirty miles north of Channel-Port aux Basques is a long, exposed, barren ridge that is notorious with Newfoundland motorists. Signs at both ends of this high place warn:

CAUTION
WIND WARNING
WINDS IN THIS AREA HAVE BEEN
RECORDED TO GUST UP TO 200 KMH
IF ANY DIFFICULTY IS EXPERIENCED IN
OPERATING YOUR VEHICLE, YOU ARE ADVISED
TO STOP UNTIL WIND SUBSIDES

There's a restaurant near here with its walls plastered with photos of trucks overturned and blown off the highway by these treacherous winds. A nearby stretch of railroad tracks is equipped with heavy chains used for tying down freight cars to prevent them from being blown over. In view of the buffeting winds we'd already encountered, we approached this area with some trepidation. I didn't tell the others, but I kept scanning the roadside ditches in fear of coming upon our trailer-truck overturned and its drivers and cargo of innocent caribou killed or maimed. But evidently our drivers had had the skill and intelligence to negotiate this deadly spot safely. There was no sign of them—even their tracks had been obliterated by the howling wind.

Having passed this point, we knew we had it made. We might even make our scheduled departure aboard the ferry boat at 11 a.m.

At mid-morning, we rolled into the ferry-loading yard at Channel-Port aux Basques. There, in the middle of the huge, nearly empty lot, was our trailer truck. We had all made it! We'd traversed that entire island, in a raging blizzard, in one long night of driving.

The ferry was set to leave at eleven. We were apprehensive because of the high winds, which we were told were blowing eighty to ninety kilometers per hour out on the water, but we resigned ourselves to the supposed good sense of the Marine Atlantic Ferry Service. In hindsight, we should have waited for the storm to pass.

McCollough and Heldenbrand fed and watered the caribou and laced their drinking water with a mild sedative in order to keep them calm during the anticipated rough crossing. We drove aboard the appropriately named the MV *Caribou*, among only a few vehicles. Several men steered us to our parking spots and secured our vehicles to the deck with heavy chains and tightening clamps. On the way over to the island, we'd been told that on a recent crossing a trailer-truck broke from its chains in a heavy sea and rattled around in the hold, smashing up several passenger cars parked next to it. This ferry crew was obviously taking no chances of a similar occurrence.

Soon the loading ramp was closed and secured, mooring lines hauled in, and the ferry began slipping down the long, winding channel to the open sea. The channel, even protected as it was, was being whipped by wind-driven whitecaps that were flinging their spray upon the town's small, scattered white houses and deserted streets.

We hadn't gone far out to sea—the flashing beacon light on the last ledge at the mouth of the harbor was still visible astern—when the 500-foot-long ferry, capable of carrying some 1,500 passengers, began to rise and plunge and heel in the sixty-foot seas and 120-kmh wind blasts. During the first hour of this, I kept expecting to hear the announcement that we were turning back because of the weather.

We made wry jokes and comments to break the tension as we rode out the hurricane-force storm. It was cold in the passenger lounge—we'd later learn there was no power left to provide heat because the vessel had been taking in a lot of water and onboard pumps were working overtime——and the few passengers kept moving around to stay warm. Eventually, we all drifted to the only place on the vessel that still had a little heat: the ship's bar. Soon there were twenty or twenty-five of us in there. We all chatted quietly. Heldenbrand pulled a couple of the padded lounge chairs together, curled up, and fell sound asleep. Lucky him. The storm raged on.

The ferry run across the Gulf of St. Lawrence from Newfoundland to Nova Scotia aboard the *Caribou* normally takes about five to six hours. After the sixth hour we were still far from shore, but we began sensing a slight lessening of the high lifts and drops of the bow. About an hour out from North Sydney, we came in the lee of the great, long cliff-sided point for which that portion of Nova Scotia is named: Cape Breton. We had made it, but at considerable cost to the caribou, as we would soon discover.

Shortly after the seas began to calm, we were told that supper was being served in the cafeteria. Here we found cooks' helpers trying to repair the chaotic evidence of our rough passage. The dining tables were anchored to the deck, and therefore still standing, but every chair in the place was on its back. Everything loose had been knocked to the floor. Worst of all, we had to step around great streaks and pools of thick, black, tarry grease that had spilled out from the floor drains and spread over large areas of the freshly carpeted floor.

A crewman suggested that we go down to the upper vehicle deck and look at the bow. What we saw was sobering. Steel plates and bolted joints were bent and crumpled. Wet streaks down the inside of the hull showed where water had forced its way in. Most disturbing was a huge channel iron, lying horizontally across the inside of the bow to reinforce the joints. This huge beam, which must have weighed tons, had bent and buckled. It was the main strength member of that bow. Fortunately it hadn't failed.

After we had disembarked in North Sidney, the storm knocked out power to the town and to a large portion of northern Nova Scotia. We followed the caribou truck through the dark and deserted streets to the Clansman Motel up on a hill above the town. There, in the candlelit lobby, a couple of pleasant ladies used flashlights to check us in. We were each given a candle and matches, and sent to our cold, dark rooms.

We had left a wake-up call for 4:30 a.m. The power came back on at 4:25. In a few minutes we were outside, loaded up, and had the vehicles started despite the bitter cold. We stopped at the first open restaurant for breakfast, and then were on the road and rolling again. It remained bitterly cold and windy, but the boat ride was behind us, the road was becoming barer and dryer the farther south and west we went, and the sun was shining. We were homeward bound and nothing could stop us now—except, as we were to discover, the ultimate barrier, more formidable than blizzards or raging seas: the federal bureaucracy.

The Big Stall

Toward midday we had traversed most of Nova Scotia and were about to enter the province of New Brunswick. We had a scheduled stop here at Sackville, at the Canadian National Agricultural Station, where the blood and other samples from the caribou had been air-lifted from St. John's each day of the captures, to take care of legal paperwork. This was expected to be more a formality than anything else because all official arrangements and agreements had been worked out previously. U.S. and Canadian officials had agreed, for example, that, since all the caribou were going to be held in an isolated pen— in effect, in quarantine—under the care of federal and state veterinarians, any disease problems that cropped up could be taken care of there.

This stop also provided an opportunity for the veterinarians to feed and water the animals and check on their condition before hitting the final leg of the journey home. With luck, we could be in Orono that very night!

But upon raising the doorway at the rear of the trailer, the doctors were confronted with a sad disappointment: Two of the caribou were down, one of which had died, trampled under the feet of the other caribou. Another, still alive, was found after examination to be too weak to save. It was removed from the truck and humanely dispatched.

The remainder of the animals on the truck, however, looked in fine shape. They were given food and fresh water. The rear of the truck was re-closed and locked. The drivers climbed aboard and wheeled out onto the highway. We still had the paperwork to tend to, so we planned to meet up with the truck for supper down the road.

But it wasn't to be so easy. Some mid-level official at the U.S. Department of Agriculture had decided that we couldn't bring the caribou into the States today. There must be a three-day lapse between the time an animal is injected with disease antibodies and the time it is checked to see if it shows a reaction indicating it carries the disease organisms. The way to determine this is for a trained veterinarian to feel for a bump at the location of the injection, near the animal's rump. A bump means the animal is infected. We knew this all in advance, and arrangements had been made to conduct the test on each animal after they had arrived at the Orono pens.

A delay would mean the already-stressed caribou would have to remain on that truck. There was no place to keep them at Sackville, and even if there was, unloading and reloading would only increase their stress. Some would not be able to survive it. Meanwhile, the truck with our precious cargo was rolling toward Maine. We had to try to catch and stop them if possible.

While Heldenbrand was on the phone, desperately pleading our case with some high official back home, I began making calls about the truck. The New Brunswick Highway Patrol advised the best way to intercept it would be to call the two truck-weighing stations along the route between Sackville and the Maine border. Since all trucks were required to stop and be weighed, we might catch them at one of these. I called, but both said the Maine caribou truck had already stopped and passed through.

In late afternoon, with the Maine congressional delegation talking with the highest levels at the U.S. Fish and Wildlife Service and the Department of Agriculture, it appeared that some progress was being made. But it took a Canadian to come up with an acceptable solution. When we first stopped in Sackville, we had unexpectedly met up with Mike Heald, one of the veterinarians who had been working with us on the caribou captures. He had flown in from St. John's earlier in the day to present a scientific paper at a convention in Halifax the next day. Heald, a certified Canadian federal veterinary inspector, offered to accompany us to Orono and personally supervise the testing of the animals. U.S. officials accepted this compromise—provided that the truck be legally sealed by customs officers before entering the United States, and that the seal be opened only by a certified veterinary inspector.

That meant I had to make more calls to the Canadian and U.S. customs offices at our port of entry, St. Stephen, New Brunswick / Calais, Maine. Both said the truck had not arrived there yet, but when it did, they would handle the sealing. I also asked the U.S. Customs agent to relay a message to the drivers to head for Orono without us.

And now began another leg of this incredible odyssey, which would have made a zany comic opera if there hadn't been so much at stake in terms of the welfare of the caribou.

Our immediate problem was how to fit Dr. Heald into our small, already-bulging-at-the-seams station wagon. Not only was he a big man and six feet tall, but he was also carrying a suitcase only slightly smaller than a steamer trunk. With some judicious rearranging, accompanied by a few curses and oaths, a place for this was finally made. There was only one seat in the car that could accommodate our genial giant: the front passenger seat. Even then, he had to twist and cramp himself in, because there was so much junk in back we couldn't move the seat all the way back. Heldenbrand and McCollough, fortunately both rather small, squeezed themselves into what space was left in the backseat. And I, of course, as the owner of the car and self-assigned chauffeur, had to occupy the driver's seat.

Yet Another Blizzard

It was dark when we finally departed Sackville. We stopped for supper at a roadside diner near Moncton, and when we emerged, it was snowing. Again, we didn't know it, but we were on a collision course with another monster northeast storm roaring up the Atlantic Coast, through the Gulf of Maine and the Bay of Fundy. December was turning into a record-breaking month for these nor'easters.

The snow intensified once we passed through St. John's. Snow is snow, you say? Not so. This snowfall was different from the one we'd driven through across Newfoundland. That was dry, cold, and whipped by the wind. This snow was heavier, wetter, and falling much faster. It was being blown in off the nearby, relatively warm ocean waters, and it was piling up fast with no snowplows in sight.

Our little car, loaded even heavier than before, was having a tough time of it. This snow was hard to push through, and I had to keep driving as hard as I dared to go; if we had to slow down or stop, especially on one of the hills, I was worried we might not get going again.

But on the brighter side, we had a new, welcome distraction. Heald, it turned out, was an amusing and enlightened entertainer. We learned that he was a Scotsman, had gone to veterinary school in Scotland, and had later moved to Canada to take up residence and start his career. In fact, he'd attended the same school as James Alfred Wight, the famous veterinarian who, under the pen name of James Herriot, wrote the *All Creature Great and Small* series of books about a Yorkshire veterinarian. Heald had, in fact, met Wight, and had spent some time in his Yorkshire dales. His tales helped to keep us entertained through that difficult evening.

We gradually drew closer to Maine. Still no sign of a Canadian snowplow. By now, the snow was deep enough that we could hear and feel it hitting and dragging on the undercarriage of the car, but that remarkable little Chevy's front wheels kept digging in and pulling us along. I kept telling the guys: "This will change when we cross into Maine. Mainers love to plow snow. You'll see: The plows will be out pushing snow all night long!" The last hill in Canada was the toughest, and we barely made it to the top. We saw streetlights at the outskirts of St. Stephen, and from there it was all downhill.

It must have been after eleven when we finally pulled into the U.S. Customs post at Calais across the St. Croix River. The agent on duty told us the caribou truck had passed through many hours before, and had been properly sealed. We were waved through and emerged onto Calais's mercifully plowed streets.

It was still snowing and blowing hard, we were still ninety-odd miles from Orono via Maine's notorious "Airline" road through the semi-wilderness of Washington County, and we were bushed. We decided the prudent thing to do was put up for the night, grab a few hours of sleep, and hit the road early.

Four-thirty a.m. came in a wink, and soon we were turning on to notorious Route 90 for the final leg of our journey. Route 90, a major—virtually the only—east-west artery in that part of the state, is one of Maine's legendary country highways. Though some of its most infamous hills and curves have been tamed by improvements made by the state highway depart-ment in recent years, it remains a potentially dangerous road, especially so in the conditions we faced that morning. Sure, it had been plowed and the snow had let up except for a few flur-ries here and there, but the heavy snow had left a slushy residue. There was no way to travel very fast under those con-ditions, and we also encountered frequent, and slow, traffic. We finally reached the campus of the University of Maine in Orono a little after seven that morning.

The topic of how to release the caribou into the pens had undergone intense discussion during planning sessions. It would be a crucial time for the animals, coming at the end of their long ordeal of captures, handling, and trucking. Therefore, their exit from the truck had to be as quiet and trauma-free as possible. It was agreed that only a handful of people, the barest minimum necessary to do the job, would be allowed into the pen area at that time. This ideal, however, was not to be, and I never found out who was responsible for this breach of planned procedure.

What we expected to find at the pens was the truck and a few veterinarians and biologists waiting quietly for us. What we found was a virtual circus. We had barely driven a quarter-mile up the access road to the pens when we encountered cars, pickups, and four-wheel-drives jammed everywhere, some parked at crazy angles with their noses rammed into the road-side brush. When we got out of our car, some distance from the pens, we heard a terrible, dreaded sound: hooves frantically beating on the floors and walls of the trailer. We'd heard that same sound at the capture site when some inadvertent sound or movement had panicked the beasts and they did what any wild creatures would instinctively do: tried to run. Any animal unfortunate or weak enough to fall would be trampled under the hooves of its panicky fellows.

Upon hearing this commotion and recognizing its implications, Heald leapt out and, on his long legs, began running toward the pen, shouting, "Things are out of control! Things are out of control!" McCollough and Heldenbrand raced up the road after him. I grabbed my video camera and recorder out of the rear of the station wagon and followed them, running as fast as my heavy load and aging lungs would permit.

At the pens, the scene was one of pandemonium. People were crowded along the fence, their faces peering over the top, and many camera lenses could be seen. Even more people were inside the compound, some crouched behind trees and wood-piles, others standing in the open with cameras. Some members of the press, who had been expressly told they would not be allowed, were in the pen, too.

All eyes were on the open gate at the rear of the truck. Every few minutes, loud shouts would ensue from inside the trailer, someone's head would appear, and a gate would partially open. Then a caribou would come thundering down the ramp and gallop into the pen, where it would dodge and duck around the assorted humanity. One far corner of the pen was free of humans; the caribou already released had gathered there, looking around, wild-eyed and agitated.

All in all, this was exactly what we had hoped to avoid.

Bucky Owen, the university's wildlife director, explained how this situation had come to be. When he and others had approached the truck early in the morning, there were no sounds coming from it. Because they had heard press accounts about how we had fought snowstorms and hurricanes at sea en route to Maine, they feared all the animals might be sick or dead. They decided not to wait for us as planned and to open the truck immediately in case they had to begin resuscitating the caribou. The people now in the truck were certified veterinarians, including two U.S. Department of Agriculture vets, and they were individually checking each animal for disease symptoms before releasing them. The animals continued coming down the ramp one at a time. After running about in some panic and confusion, they'd stop and join their mates at the far corner. In all, twenty-three caribou came down the ramp into the pen. They looked in remarkably good shape considering all that had happened in their lives over the past few days.

Two caribou were found on the floor of the trailer, too weak to stand on their own. Both had large, gaping wounds on their backs from trampling hooves. They were taken to a nearby shed and treated. They seemed to respond at first and it was hoped they would recover, but both died later in the day.

Meeting the Natives

For the next couple of weeks, the world was shut off from the caribou pen. Only McCollough and a few helpers looked after the caribou. In almost daily telephone conversations, Mark assured me the caribou seemed to be adapting.

On the weekend just before Christmas, the university opened the area up to the public, and Mainers, their curiosity piqued, came out in force. Despite bitter, near-zero temperatures, some 3,500 people walked in on the access road to stand quietly at the pen gate and look at their state's newest residents. Most expressed surprise and delight upon their first look. They were intrigued most by the caribous' big, splayed hooves, and by their light coloration. The gentle, placid caribou showed much interest in their visitors as well; several wandered up to the fence gate to get a closer look. For many Mainers, it was love at first sight. Donations to the Transplant Fund rolled in.

Money—or rather, the lack thereof—was a constant worry to McCollough. The donations still mostly came in the form of small contributions from individuals, social clubs, and school kids. Fund-raising dinners were held, and when I got the first draft of the documentary videotape completed, corporation members began taking it around and showing it to groups and gatherings. Still, the costs kept mounting, and the contributions barely kept up.

One of the more successful money-raising efforts was led by McCollough himself. A talented artist, he drew a striking portrait of a magnificent caribou stag, which was printed as a poster and sold in a limited edition. Another innovative fund-raising move was the "Adopt-a-Caribou" program. For $2,500, the cost of supporting one caribou for a year, groups or individuals could adopt a caribou and give it a name. One of the first communities to do so was also one of Maine's smallest. School kids in the tiny community of Eustis, near the Quebec border, adopted a caribou and named it "Eustis." The city of Caribou, naturally, adopted a caribou. So did a Bangor television station and the employees of a Portland meatpacking company, Jordan Meats, whose president was a member of the caribou corporation.

Though the bulk of the herd was doing well in the pen on the pellet food (a mixture of grain and alfalfa used successfully on caribou elsewhere, supplemented with lichens, minerals, and vitamins), one of the three stags remained thin and failed to respond. Strangely, it's the biggest, strongest caribou that have the greatest difficulty surviving the winters. Throughout the fall breeding season, they are constantly fighting with other males and servicing their harems of from ten to twenty females. This goes on day and night for weeks and takes a lot of energy. They have little time or desire to feed. Often, the fights leave them with serious injuries. Little wonder, then, that they enter the winter in an already severely stressed condition.

Caribou, like all ruminants, need bacteria in their stomachs to help digest food. A shift in diet can disrupt this bacterial colony. This particular stag had lost its bacteria and was unable to process its food. It died in the pen. Another stag, though it remained thin, survived the winter and regained its weight and strength in the spring. So now there were two stags, and twenty does.

Winter waned, but not the interest. The university opened the pens to the public one Saturday a month until early spring and the approach of the calving time. A donation box kept at the pen gate picked up several hundred dollars each time the public was allowed to visit.

New Arrivals

Female caribou normally drop their fawns from mid-May until early June. At the peak, the calves come fast. The calving is concentrated in a small time period as a means of foiling predators. With so many calves appearing in such a short time, predators can kill and eat only a small percentage. Within a few hours, caribou calves are able to follow their mothers, however awkward they appear on their long, spindly legs. In a few days, they can keep up with the running adults.

I was asked to provide pool video coverage of the first births. By mid-May, Mark and I were on edge. Virtually each day, McCollough would call me with a report on the progress—or rather, the lack thereof—toward producing our first calf. I stayed close to home on weekends. We waited. Concerns were mounting. There were hints that perhaps the journey down from Newfoundland had been too strenuous and stressing and had caused the pregnant does to abort during the trip or after reaching Maine.

On an evening in late May, the call finally came from McCollough.

"Can you come in the morning? I just left the pen and we have two calves!"

I left home early the next day for the hundred-mile drive to Orono. My video camera was warmed up and ready to roll when McCollough met me at the pen gate. Just inside, next to a freshly cut tree stump, was the baby caribou. It lay very still and quiet. I focused and began taping. Soon the mother, who had been standing some yards away, walked toward the calf. She stopped, and made some deep, grunting sounds. The calf got up onto its long, spindly legs and began walking toward her, affording me an excellent video sequence of its awkward gait. Its rear legs seemed far too long for the rest of its body, but it gamely followed along as mother led it over to a quiet corner.

We eased our way to where one of McCollough's favorite does had gone to have her calf. (McCollough knew her to be very tame and tolerant of humans.) She stood placidly over her offspring, which was sleeping at her feet. Every few minutes she'd put her head down to sniff and nuzzle the amazing little bundle of fur and limpid brown eyes. We got to within some twenty feet of the pair and I began filming. With the zoom lens, I was able to fill the entire frame with the sleeping youngster. It was curled up into a neat little tuck, its sides moving rhythmically as it breathed quietly in peaceful sleep.

After a while, the doe laid down beside the calf. She smelled, nuzzled, and licked the calf as it lay under her throat. It was a classic scene of maternal devotion, as she patiently and contentedly tended to her youngster. For a long time she remained lying at its side, in a semi-doze. It was quiet and peaceful in the early-morning light under the trees. Overhead, chickadees buzzed busily among the branches, looking for tiny seeds. It was, for me, a special, magical time that I'll never forget.

During the next week or so, the caribou were left alone except for daily replenishment of feed. The number of babies increased daily, until sixteen were born. At first, all seemed fine, but then five calves suddenly became sick and died before the veterinarians could administer any help. The doctors uncovered the problem: The calves' umbilical cords had become infected from the caribou feces covering the ground of the pen, and the infection had made its way to their body cavities, where it raged and consumed the tiny calves. Such an infection is not uncommon to cattle. The preventive, once the problem was diagnosed, was to simply coat the umbilical cords with iodine as soon as possible after birth. McCollough and the vets also resolved that in future springs, a special "clean" pen would be set aside for a birthing and nursery area. Those measures prevented a recurrence of the sickness.

Another setback during the first calving season was the unusually high ratio of males to females. After the five calves had died, we were left with four young females and seven young males, not a good ratio when you consider that in the wild, one stag can service ten to twenty does.

Through the early summer, all of the caribou did well. The calves were growing, shedding their "baby fur" of beige and taking on their mothers' dark summer coloration. (The caribou's summer coat is very thin, allowing its black skin to show through.) They were thriving on a diet of special grains and other forage. The male calves were beginning to grow stubs of antlers, which were expected to reach six to eight inches long by late fall.

By midsummer, the two stags' antlers were growing fast and were covered in a velvety skin containing the blood vessels supplying them nourishment. In mid-August the two stags sported tremendous sets of antlers. The largest stag, weighing about 450 pounds, had a rare "double shovel" set.

Caribou offspring in a pen at Orono.

In mid-August, the university announced that more than 20,000 visitors had come to the pens to view the caribou.

The First Breeding

In October, McCollough's calls to me were tinged with more excitement than ever. The stags, which he called Burgeo and Lowell, were now magnificent, he said. They had completely rubbed off the velvet covering their antlers, a sign they were ready to rut, and they were stalking about their harems in regal splendor.

In mid-October I took the video camera and went up to Orono to see them for myself. McCollough was right; they were a sight to behold. Burgeo, the bigger, more dominant of the two males, was exerting his dominance by trying to keep all the females to himself, and fighting off the more submissive Lowell. According to McCollough, the two stags engaged in some major battles, all of which Lowell lost. Burgeo was successfully keeping Lowell from breeding, which is not good genetics. It's best to spread the gene pool among more than one male. So a fence was erected to separate the main pen, and ten does and their calves were placed in each pen with each of the males. This didn't satisfy Burgeo, however. Several times he knocked the fence down and stole away all of Lowell's females. The barrier had to be re-erected and reinforced.

By early November, McCollough felt that Burgeo and Lowell had done their duties diligently during the mating season. Normally, 80 percent of adult females get bred each year, and McCollough was looking for at least another fifteen new calves in the spring.

As winter and the first anniversary of the capture arrived, McCollough and the Maine Caribou Transplant Corporation could look back upon a successful first year. They were raising enough money to cover the bills, and despite setbacks, they had thirty healthy caribou. They began to look for potential release sites in anticipation of the first release of caribou to the wild in the spring of 1989.

The Tragic Conclusion

The caribou were eventually taken some 100 miles north and released at two separate locations, one in Baxter State Park, and the other just outside the park boundaries. The sites were chosen for their remoteness, ideal habitat, and small deer populations. But it was all for naught.

Shortly after their release, the caribou began dying. Each caribou had been fitted with a radio collar prior to release. These had been programmed to change signals after an interval if the collar stopped moving—as in after death. Biologists with radio receivers went into the woods and located each of the dead animals. In virtually all cases, those caribou were determined to have *P. tenuis* brainworm. Many appeared to have been killed by bears, or at least scavenged by bears and coyotes, perhaps while weakened and vulnerable in the late stages of sickness.

What happened? During the period that the caribou were staying in the Orono pens, they had been receiving medicine in their feed to suppress or kill *P. tenuis*. Evidently, the parasite was able to survive in a latent state and was revived to do its lethal damage after the caribou were released and no longer receiving the medicine. Because *P. tenuis* is carried by deer, the site selected for keeping the caribou at Orono, in hindsight, was possibly the worst possible choice: It has an extremely high deer population.

Soon all of the caribou were dead, as were the dreams of restoring caribou in and near Baxter, where the last native caribou had also been last seen. And, after two costly failed attempts, it's unlikely those dreams will ever again be revived.

What impact did this project have on me? After seeing them on their native range in Newfoundland, I became hooked on the caribou. As Canadian wildlife biologist Shane Mahoney said, "When you see coming from the distance a mature male caribou in his fall breeding regalia, you are impressed. . . . [It] is one of the most stunning wild animals imaginable." To see one of these proud males, with polished antlers held high, is to see wilderness personified. It would have been magnificent to have these animals back in the wilds of Maine.

If nothing else, this experience gave me the opportunity to meet and work with some remarkable people: doctors McCollough and Heldenbrand, Bucky Owen, and Canadians Shane Mahoney, Eugene Mercer, Rob Greenwood, Con Finlay, and their colleagues.

It was an experience I wouldn't want to have missed.

What Do They Do All Winter?

When we lived year-round at Brassua Lake, my wife, Anita, and I were constantly asked by our summer sports, "But what in the world do you people do up here all winter?"

Here's what I'd tell them:

We live a good piece from the nearest power line, so we have no electric lights. We use kerosene and gas lamps. No TV, no electric blankets. No thermostatically controlled central heating; we burn wood. No automatic washer. No hot or cold running water. Our summertime water source, a large spring on the ridge up back, is too far away to permit burying the pipe to prevent it from freezing. We carry our water.

Our access road isn't plowed in the winter. We leave our car at the main highway and snowshoe in and out. All incoming and outgoing supplies are conveyed by a "moose sled," a king-size hand sled, or by toboggan. We do have a telephone and a battery-powered radio, which keep us in touch with the world.

Shocking, you say? This is primitive living? We're too busy—and happy—to realize it.

Just taking care of our normal daily chores—carrying in water and wood, tending fires and what-not—consumes a good portion of each day. As I said, we burn wood for heat, and our

189

camp guests love a good wood fire—all of which uses up a mountain of firewood annually, which must be replaced. The trees must be selected, felled, limbed, sawed, and split, and the wood stacked up so it won't get lost under a new snowfall. Then it has to be sledded down to the woodshed, tossed in, tiered up for drying, and finally, carried into the house and cabins for burning. Wasn't it Thoreau who said that heating with wood warms you twice—once when you cut it, and again when you burn it? Did he only say twice?

When we run out of other things to do, there's always snow to shovel from around doorways, paths, and off the cabin and outbuilding roofs so they won't cave in under its weight. And we're in the unique position of receiving snow from two angles, vertically and horizontally. We live near the southeast end of a nine-mile-long lake, and the prevailing wind is westerly and it loves to blow. Consequently, we eventually wind up with most of the snow that falls on the lake, too. It piles up around the place in mountainous drifts and, by late winter, it takes a Swiss mountaineer to pick his way from cabin to cabin.

One winter, our total snowfall measured an official 12 feet, 11 ⅞ inches, a record for the area. Before that winter was out, I was actually shoveling snow from the roofs and throwing it up onto the snowdrifts!

When our summer guests discover that we spend our winters here, they ask, "But aren't you snowbound most of the winter?" Snowbound? We've never been snowbound for more than a few hours at a time. Snow is an ancient foe up here. The natives are used to it, they expect it, and they know how to handle it. At worst, it's an inconvenience.

Take for example, a recent bad snowstorm. An eighteen-inch nor'easter, it clobbered the entire Atlantic shore before blitzing us. While we were enjoying breakfast the next morning, the radio brought us an appealing picture of the storm's wake. All the major cities from Washington, D.C., north were paralyzed and would be for several days. Highways were buried under snowdrifts, thousands of cars had been abandoned. Several people perished from over-exertion while shoveling snow and wrestling with stuck vehicles.

After breakfast, I spent a couple of hours doing some essential shoveling around the place and tramped over the paths with my snowshoes. (Fresh snow on a path, packed down in this manner, will freeze to a concrete-like consistency after a couple of sub-zero nights. It saves a lot of shoveling!) Late in the forenoon, deciding to run into town to pick up the mail and supplies, I snowshoed up to the car, where I found the highway department had already plowed the road. I had just started digging into the snowbank across the end of the driveway when a kind-hearted fellow came along on a plow-equipped tractor. Several swipes of the blade and my driveway was cleared. Thirty minutes after leaving the house, I was rolling into town, where I found life going on much as usual.

Lest you get the impression that our life is a constant back-breaking round of all work and no play, let me hasten to dispel your fears. We do have our pleasures, simple though they may seem to the cosmopolitan mind.

One of the most popular winter pastimes is ice-fishing. Practically everyone in the area is an avid member of the red-nosed fraternity, and our large lakes draw frostbitten devotees from all over the state. Fish houses dot the lakes as long as the fishing season is open, and I usually set up a couple of shacks of my own.

Another favorite pastime, especially for our dog, Rusty (mostly cocker spaniel), is spying on the wildlife around the house. Anita religiously keeps the large feeding station just outside the living room window well-stocked, and it attracts an endless variety of chickadees, nuthatches, woodpeckers, jays, and red squirrels. Most every winter evening a friendly family of flying squirrels swoops down to liven things up. Foxes prowl the backyard and persist in enraging Rusty by digging up her bones and other treasures. Owls hoot on the ridge up back. Snowshoe hares hop in and out of the brush at the edge of the woods. Who needs TV?

Paul Fournier

March 1958 at Brassua Lake.

One of the pleasantest ways I know to spend a few winter hours is to don my snowshoes and slip into the woods. There, in the muffled solitude of the snow-draped forest, I'm treated to rare glimpses of our furred and feathered neighbors' eternal struggle for survival.

How do we spend those long, cold winter evenings? Once or twice a week we exchange visits with our nearest neighbors, Faye and Lee Foss, who live at Brassua Dam, for a spirited evening of cards. (When folks will snowshoe through the woods in sub-zero weather to spend an evening with you, they can be considered good friends.) Occasionally, we drive into Rockwood to spend an evening with friends there.

Mostly, though, we spend our evenings at home, listening to the radio and reading or working on some simple task. There's something strangely comforting and soul-satisfying about sitting safely and cozily in your cabin in the wilderness, warmed by a stove filled with wood which you yourself have cut, while the temperature outside drops way below zero and the wind howls and tears at the building. You feel as if you're facing the worst nature can throw at you, and you're winning.

What do we do up here all winter? Besides working, playing, fishing, and making love, we're living—and enjoying it!

A version of this chapter was first published in *Yankee* magazine.

About the Author

Paul J. Fournier is a native Mainer with a long career in the Maine woods, starting out as a Registered Maine Guide, bush pilot, and owner of a sporting camp business on Brassua Lake. For twenty years he was the public information officer for the Maine Department of Inland Fisheries and Wildlife. He also produced a weekly television program, *Maine Fish and Wildlife*, for the Maine Public Broadcasting Network. He has written and photographed extensively for a number of magazines, including *Audubon*, *Natural History*, *National Geographic*, *Country Gentleman*, *Yankee*, *Down East*, *Field & Stream*, and *Outdoor Life*, among others. In recent years he has written exclusively for several aviation magazines. He divides his time between Maine and Florida.